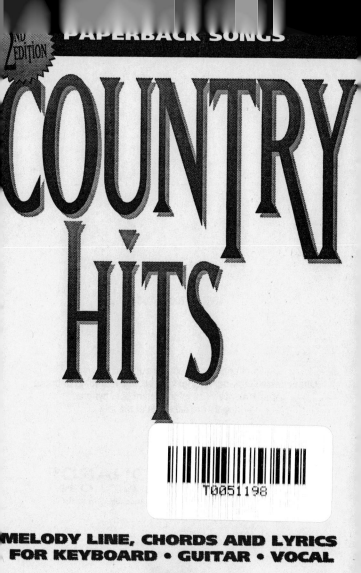

2ND EDITION

PAPERBACK SONGS

COUNTRY HITS

MELODY LINE, CHORDS AND LYRICS FOR KEYBOARD • GUITAR • VOCAL

HAL•LEONARD•

ISBN 0-7935-5258-3

For all works contained herein:
Unauthorized copying, arranging, adapting, recording or public
performance is an infringement of copyright.
Infringers are liable under the law.

HAL•LEONARD®
CORPORATION
7777 W. BLUEMOUND RD. P.O. BOX 13819 MILWAUKEE, WI 53213

Visit Hal Leonard Online at
www.halleonard.com

Welcome to the PAPERBACK SONGS SERIES.

Do you play piano, guitar, electronic keyboard, sing or play any instrument for that matter? If so, this handy "pocket tune" book is for you.

The concise, one-line music notation consists of:

MELODY, LYRICS & CHORD SYMBOLS

Whether strumming the chords on guitar, "faking" an arrangement on piano/keyboard or singing the lyrics, these fake book style arrangements can be enjoyed at any experience level – hobbyist to professional.

The musical skills necessary to successfully use this book are minimal. If you play guitar and need some help with chords, a basic chord chart is included at the back of the book.

While playing and singing is the first thing that comes to mind when using this book, it can also serve as a compact, comprehensive reference guide.

However you choose to use this PAPERBACK SONGS SERIES book, by all means have fun!

CONTENTS

(contents continued)

AIN'T GOIN' DOWN
('Til the Sun Comes Up)

Words and Music by KIM WILLIAMS,
GARTH BROOKS and KENT BLAZY

Bright Country

Copyright © 1993 Sony/ATV Tunes LLC, Major Bob Music Co., Inc.,
No Fences Music, Inc. and Careers-BMG Music Publishing, Inc.
All Rights on behalf of Sony/ATV Tunes LLC Administered by Sony/ATV Music Publishing,
8 Music Square West, Nashville, TN 37203
International Copyright Secured   All Rights Reserved

scream-ing out a warn-ing: "Girl, you'd bet-ter get your red head
and park down by the creek, where it's George Strait 'til real late and

1

back in bed be-fore the morn-ing."
danc-ing cheek to cheek.

2

They Ain't Go-ing Down 'til the

sun comes up, ain't giv-ing in 'til they

get e-nough. Go-ing 'round the world in a

pick-up truck.

Ain't Go-ing Down 'til the sun comes up.

Ten 'til twelve is wine and danc-ing.
Six o'-clock on Sat-ur-day, her

Mid-night starts the hard ro-manc-ing.
folks don't know he's on his way. The

C

One o' - clock that truck is rock - ing.
stalls are clean, the hors - es fed. They

G

Two is com - ing, still no stop - ping.
say she's ground - ed 'til she's dead. Well,

D

Break to check the clock at three. They're
here he comes a - round the bend,

right at where they wan - ta be and
slow - ing down. She's jump - ing in.

G

four o' - clock get up and go - ing.
Hey, Mom, your daugh - ter's gone and

𝄋𝄋

Five o'-clock that roost-er's crow-ing. Hey._____
there they go a - gain. Hey. _____ *(Instrumental solo each time)*

C   ⌐ 3 ⌐   **G**

D |¹ **G**

(Solo ends) Yeah, they

|² **G**   D.S. al Coda   **CODA** ⊕ #

(Solo ends) They

D.S.S. and Fade
G 𝄐

sun comes up.   Yeah.

ALL MY EX'S LIVE IN TEXAS

Words and Music by LYNDIA J. SHAFER
and SANGER D. SHAFER

Country Shuffle

All my ex-'s live in Tex-as,

and Tex-as is a place.

I'd dear-ly love to be.

But all my ex-'s live in

Tex-as, (1.,2.) and that's (D.C.) there-

why I hang my hat in Ten-nes-

Copyright © 1986 by Acuff-Rose Music, Inc.
All Rights Reserved Used by Permission

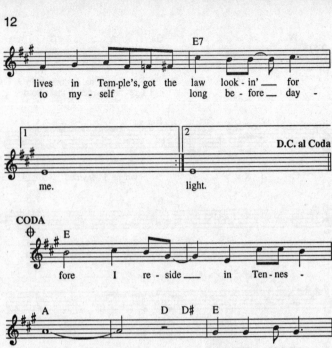

lives   in   Tem-ple's, got the   law   look-in' ___ for
to   my - self   long   be - fore ___ day -

me.   light.

D.C. al Coda

CODA

fore   I   re - side ___ in   Ten - nes -

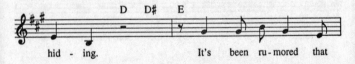

see. _____   Some   folks   think   I'm

hid - ing.   It's   been   ru - mored   that

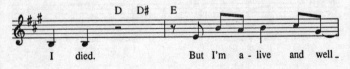

I   died.   But   I'm   a - live   and   well _

_____ in   Ten - nes -   see.

ALMOST GOODBYE

**Words and Music by BILLY LIVSEY
and DON SCHLITZ**

Moderately slow, in 2

There was rain on the street last night.
Now there was sun on the blinds this morn-ing

We stood be-neath the front ___ door light. ___
when I o - pened up ___ my eyes. ___

Ev - 'ry-thing we said, ___ we made
Out - side I could hear a mock - ing -

sure the neigh - bors heard. ___
bird. ___

You called me this, I called you that,
I could feel your heart - beat

stand-ing on the wel - come mat. ___
as you laid there by ___ my side. ___

Copyright © 1993 RONDOR MUSIC (LONDON) LTD.,
BMG SONGS, INC. and NEW DON SONGS
All Rights for RONDOR MUSIC (LONDON) LTD.
in the USA and Canada Administered by IRVING MUSIC, INC.
All Rights Reserved   Used by Permission

14

Ev - 'ry-thing we felt,____ it all____ came
I thought of how the world__ could end__ with

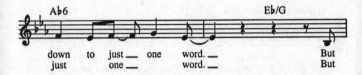

down to just__ one word.____ But
just one__ word.____ But

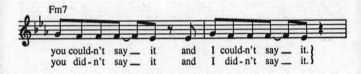

you could-n't say__ it and I could-n't say__ it.
you did-n't say__ it and I did-n't say__ it.

You know____ I tried____ my best.

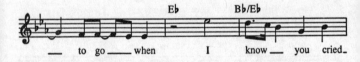

____ to go____ when I know__ you cried__

__ 'cause I hurt__ you so.____

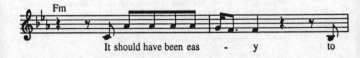

It should have been eas - y to

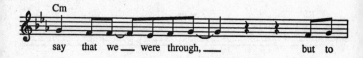

say that we __ were through, __ but to

walk a - way __ from {love _____ / love __ that way} was __

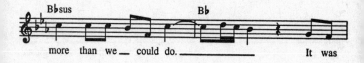

more than we __ could do. _____ It was

al - most good - bye. __

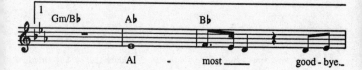

Al - most __ good - bye. __

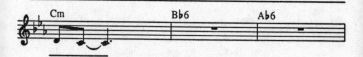

It was __ al -

most ____ good-bye. _____

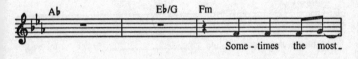

Some - times the most _

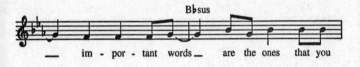

_ im - por - tant words _ are the ones that you

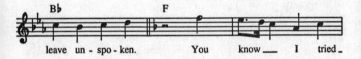

leave un - spo - ken. You know _ I tried _

_ my best _ to go _ when I

know _____ you cried _____ 'cause I hurt _

— you — so. — It should have been eas -

— y to say that we — were through, —

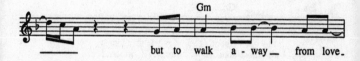

— but to walk a - way — from love —

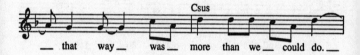

— that way — was — more than we — could do. —

— It was — al - most — good - bye. —

— Al -

Repeat ad lib. and Fade

most — good - bye. —

ALWAYS ON MY MIND

Words and Music by WAYNE THOMPSON,
MARK JAMES and JOHNNY CHRISTOPHER

Slow and steady

(1., 3.) May - be I did-n't treat ___ you
(2.) May - be I did-n't hold ___ you

quite as good ___ as I should have,
all those lone - ly, lone-ly times, ___

May - be I did-n't love ___ you
and I guess nev-er told ___ you

quite as of - ten as I should ___ have;
I'm so hap - py that you're mine; ___

Lit - tle things I should have said ___ and done,
If I made you feel ___ sec - ond best,

I just nev - er took the time. ___
girl, I'm so sor - ry I was blind. ___

© 1971 (Renewed 1999), 1979 SCREEN GEMS-EMI MUSIC INC. and SEBANINE MUSIC, INC.
All Rights Controlled and Administered by SCREEN GEMS-EMI MUSIC INC.
All Rights Reserved International Copyright Secured Used by Permission

AMAZED

Words and Music by MARV GREEN,
CHRIS LINDSEY and AIMEE MAYO

Moderately slow Country Ballad

Ev-'ry time our eyes meet, this feel-in' in-side me
The smell of your skin, the taste of your kiss,

is al-most more _ than I _ can take. _
the way you whis-per in _ the dark _

Ba-by, when you touch me,
Your hair all a-round me;

I can feel how much you love me,
ba-by, you sur-round me.

and it just blows me a - way.
You touch ev-'ry place _ in my _ heart. _

I've nev-er been _ this close _ to
Oh, it feels _ like the

Copyright © 1998 by Careers-BMG Music Publishing, Inc., Silverkiss Music Publishing,
Songs Of Nashville DreamWorks, Warner-Tamerlane Publishing Corp. and Golden Wheat Music
All Rights for Silverkiss Music Publishing Administered by Careers-BMG Music Publishing, Inc.
All Rights for Songs Of Nashville DreamWorks Administered by Cherry River Music Co.
All Rights for Golden Wheat Music Administered by Warner-Tamerlane Publishing Corp.
International Copyright Secured All Rights Reserved

Gb   E

- er.   Ev-'ry lit-tle thing that you do,—

1 Gb

— ba-by, I'm a-mazed— by you.—

Ab

—

2 Gb

— ba-by, I'm a-mazed— by you.—

Ab

(Instrumental)

B   Db   Ab

B   Gb   Dbsus

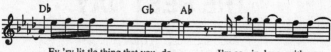

Db   Gb   Ab

— Ev-'ry lit-tle thing that you do. ___ I'm so in love_ with you._

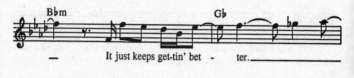

Bbm   Gb

— It just keeps get-tin' bet - ter. _____

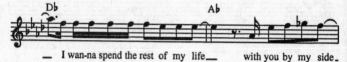

Db   Ab

— I wan-na spend the rest of my life___ with you by my side_

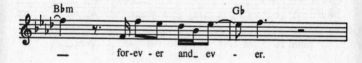

Bbm   Gb

— for-ev - er and_ ev - er.

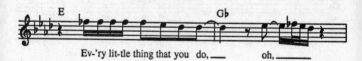

E   Gb

Ev-'ry lit-tle thing that you do, ___ oh, _____

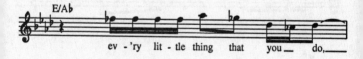

E/Ab

ev -'ry lit - tle thing that you_ do,___

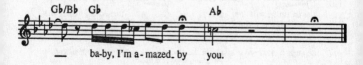

Gb/Bb Gb   Ab

— ba-by, I'm a-mazed_ by   you.

THE BEST DAY

Words and Music by DEAN DILLON
and CARSON CHAMBERLAIN

Moderately

We load-ed up__ my old sta-tion wag-on with a
fif-teenth birth-day__ rolled a-round,__

tent, a Cole-man and sleep-in' bags, some
clas-sic cars were his thing. When I

fish-in' poles,__ a cool-er of Cokes.__
pulled in the drive with that old__ Vette,__ I

Three days be-fore we had__ to be back. When you're
thought that boy__ would go__ in-sane. When you're

sev-en, you're in sev-enth heav-en when you're go-in' camp-
in your__ teens,__ your dreams__ re-volve__ a-round__

-in'in the wild out-doors. As we turned off on__ that
__ four spin-nin' wheels. We worked nights on end__ till it was

Copyright © 1999 by Acuff-Rose Music, Inc., Universal - Songs Of PolyGram International, Inc.
and Everything I Love Music
All Rights Reserved   Used by Permission

old dirt road,. he looked at me _ and swore,
new a - gain.. And as he sat be - hind_ the wheel, he said,}

"Dad, this could _ be ____ the best _ day of _ my life._

_ I've been dream - in' day_ and night_

_ a - bout the fun {we'll have.} {we've had.} Just

me and you, ___ do-in' what I've al - ways want-ed to._

_ I'm the luck - i - est boy_ a - live._

_ This is the best day of my life."

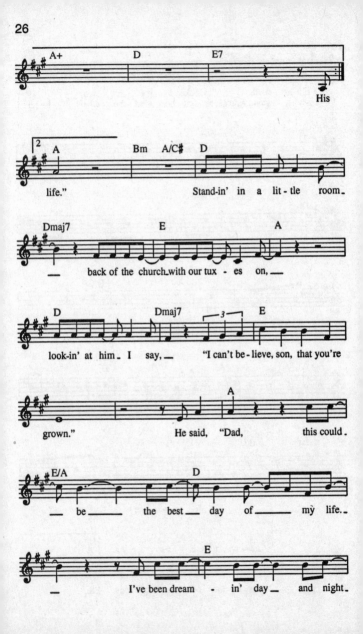

of be-in' like you. And now it's

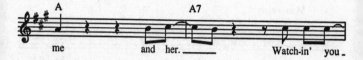

me and her. ___ Watch-in' you ___

___ and Mom, I've learned ___ I'm the luck -

- i-est man ___ a - live. ___ This is the

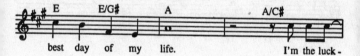

best day of my life. I'm the luck -

- i-est man ___ a - live. ___ This is the best day of my

life."

BEST OF INTENTIONS

Words and Music by
TRAVIS TRITT

I had big plans _ for our fu - ture. Said I'd
some peo-ple think _ I'm a los - er 'cause _

give you the whole _ world some-how. I
I sel-dom get _ things right. _ But

tried mak-in' good _ on that prom - ise. Thought I'd
you make me feel _ like a win - ner when you

be so much fur - ther by now.
wrap me in your _ arms so tight.

Nev - er could build _ you a cas - tle, e - ven though _
Please tell me you _ will re-mem - ber, no _

_ you're the queen _ of my heart. _ But
mat - ter how much _ I do wrong, _ that

Copyright © 2000 Post Oak Publishing, Inc.
International Copyright Secured All Rights Reserved

I've had the best __ of in - ten - tions from the start. __
I had the best __ of in - ten - tions all a - long. __

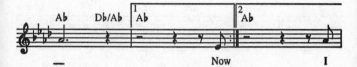

__ Now I

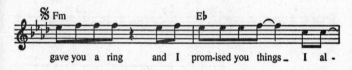

gave you a ring and I prom-ised you things __ I al -

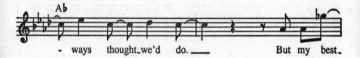

- ways thought __ we'd do. __ But my best. __

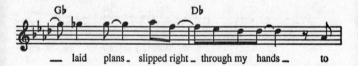

__ laid plans __ slipped right __ through my hands __ to

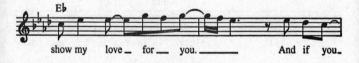

show my love __ for __ you. __ And if you. __

__ could read __ my heart, then you'd know. __

30

with-out__ ex - cep - tion   it was all__

To Coda ⊕

with the best ____ of __ in-ten - tions.

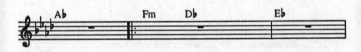

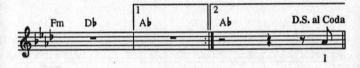

D.S. al Coda

I

CODA
⊕

So here I am ask - ing for-give -

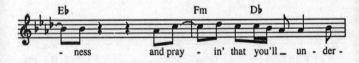

- ness   and pray - in' that you'll __ un - der -

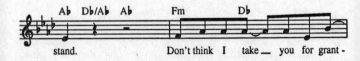

stand.   Don't think I take __ you for grant -

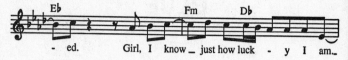

-ed.   Girl, I know _ just how luck - y I am_

_ Though you de - serve.so much bet - ter,   you won't_

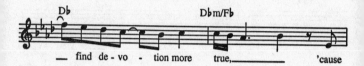

_ find de - vo - tion more   true,_____   'cause

I've had the best _ of in - ten - tions,   girl, _ I've_

_ had the best _ of in - ten - tions,   yes,

I've had the best _ of in - ten - tions lov - in' you._

BLUE

Words and Music by
BILL MACK

Moderately

Blue, _____

____ oh, so lone - some for ____ you.

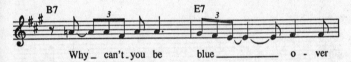

Why _ can't _ you be blue _____ o - ver

me? Blue, _____
Instrumental solo

_____ oh, so

lone - some for ____ you. Tears fill my ____ eyes _

Copyright © 1966 by Fort Knox Music Inc. and Trio Music Company, Inc.
Copyright Renewed
International Copyright Secured All Rights Reserved
Used by Permission

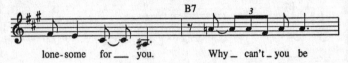

lone-some for ___ you. Why ___ can't ___ you be

D.S. al Coda

blue _____ o - ver me?

CODA

lies. _____ Blue, _____

oh, so

lone-some for ___ you. Why ___ can't ___ you be

blue _____ o - ver me?

Why ___ can't ___ you be blue _____ o - ver ___

me? _____

BOOT SCOOTIN' BOOGIE

Words and Music by
RONNIE DUNN

Moderate Shuffle

Out in the coun - try past the
got a good job, I work hard
(Instrumental solo)
bar - ten - der asks me, says,

cit - y lim - it sign, ____ well there's a
for my mon - ey. When it's
"Son, what will it be?" I want a

hon - ky tonk ____ near the coun - ty line. ____ The
quit - in' time, ____ I hit the door run - nin'. I
shot at that red-head yon - der look - in' at me. ____ The

joint starts jump - in' ev - 'ry night when the sun ____ goes
fire up my pick - up truck and let the hors - es
dance floor's hop - pin' and it's hot - ter than the Fourth of Ju -

down. ____ They got whis -
run. ____ I go fly -
ly. ____ I see out -

Copyright © 1991 Sony/ATV Songs LLC
All Rights Administered by Sony/ATV Music Publishing, 8 Music Square West, Nashville, TN 37203
International Copyright Secured All Rights Reserved

boo-gie.   Oh, —

get down   turn a - round, —   go to town, — Boot Scoot-in'

Boo - gie. _____

Woh, —   I ___ said,

get down,   turn a - round, —   go to town, — Boot Scoot-in'

Boo - gie. _____   Woh, —

get down,   turn a - round, —   go to town, — Boot Scoot-in'

Boo - gie. _____

BLUE EYES CRYING IN THE RAIN

Words and Music by
FRED ROSE

In the twi-light glow I see her. _____ blue eyes
cry-ing in the rain. _____ As we kissed good-bye and
part-ed, _____ I knew we'd nev-er meet a-gain. _____

Now my hair has turned to sil-ver. _____ All my
life I've loved in vain. _____ I can see her star in
heav-en, _____ blue eyes cry-ing in the rain. _____

Copyright © 1945 (Renewed 1973) by Milene Music, Inc.
All Rights Reserved Used by Permission

BORN TO FLY

Words and Music by SARA EVANS,
DARRELL SCOTT and MARCUS HUMMON

Copyright © 2000 by Chuck Wagon Gourmet Music, Famous Music Corporation, Sony/ATV Songs LLC,
Careers-BMG Music Publishing, Inc. and Floyd's Dream Music
All Rights on behalf of Sony/ATV Songs LLC Administered by Sony/ATV Music Publishing,
8 Music Square West, Nashville, TN 37203
All Rights on behalf of Floyd's Dream Music Administered by Careers-BMG Music Publishing, Inc.
International Copyright Secured   All Rights Reserved

But,
Oh, } how do you wait for _ heav-

-en, _ and who has that much _

time? And how do you keep your

feet on _ the ground _ when _ you know_

that you were born, _____

you were born to fly? _

My

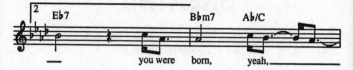

you were born, yeah,____

you were born to fly?____

So

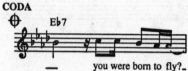

CODA

you were born to fly?.____

Fly,__ fly,__ fly._____

Hey.____

Ooh.____

BREATHE

Words and Music by HOLLY LAMAR
and STEPHANIE BENTLEY

Copyright © 1999 Cal IV Songs, Universal - Songs of PolyGram International, Inc. and Hopechest Music
All Rights on behalf of Cal IV Songs Administered by Cal IV Entertainment, Inc.,
808 19th Avenue South, Nashville, TN 37203
All Rights Reserved   Used by Permission

All my thoughts just seem to set - tle on
In a way I know my heart is wak-

- the breeze
- ing up

when I'm ly - in' wrapped up in your arms.
as all the walls come tum - bling down.

The whole world just fades a - way, the on -
Clos - er I've ev - er felt be - fore,

- ly thing I hear is the
and I know and you know there's no

beat - ing of your heart.
need for words right now.

'Cause I can feel you

breathe, it's wash-ing o - ver me, and sud-den - ly I'm

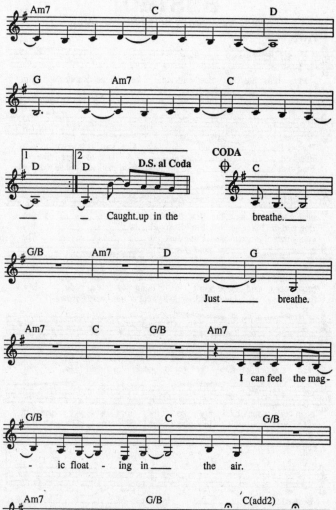

Caught up in the breathe.___

Just ___ breathe.

I can feel the mag-

- ic float - ing in ___ the air.

Be - in'___ with you ___ gets me that way.

BUSTED

Words and Music by HARLAND HOWARD

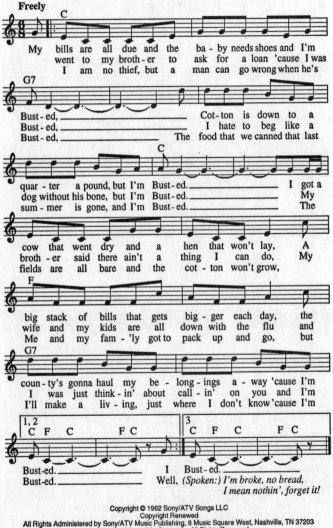

Copyright © 1962 Sony/ATV Songs LLC
Copyright Renewed
All Rights Administered by Sony/ATV Music Publishing, 8 Music Square West, Nashville, TN 37203
International Copyright Secured   All Rights Reserved

CHATTAHOOCHEE

Words and Music by JIM McBRIDE
and ALAN JACKSON

Copyright © 1992 Sony/ATV Tunes LLC, Seventh Son Music and Mattie Ruth Musick
All Rights on behalf of Sony/ATV Tunes LLC Administered by Sony/ATV Music Publishing,
8 Music Square West, Nashville, TN 37203
International Copyright Secured   All Rights Reserved

F

talk-ing 'bout cars and dream-in' 'bout wom-en.

D7   G

Nev-er had a plan; just a liv-in' for the min-ute.

C

(Solo ends) Yeah, way down yon-der on the

Chat-ta-hoo-chee; nev-er knew how much that mud-dy wa-ter

G   C

meant to me. But I learned how to swim and I

To Coda ⊕

learned who I was; a lot a-bout liv-in' and a

[1]
G   C

lit-tle 'bout love. *(Instrumental)*

G   C

BY THE TIME I GET
TO PHOENIX

Words and Music by
JIMMY WEBB

© 1967 (Renewed 1995) EMI SOSAHA MUSIC INC. and JONATHAN THREE MUSIC
All Rights Reserved International Copyright Secured Used by Permission

COLD, COLD HEART

Words and Music by
HANK WILLIAMS

Copyright © 1951 (Renewed 1979) by Acuff-Rose Music, Inc. and Hiriam Music in the U.S.A.
All Rights for Hiriam Music Administered by Rightsong Music Inc.
All Rights outside the U.S.A. Controlled by Acuff-Rose Music, Inc.
All Rights Reserved Used by Permission

oth - er love be - fore my time made
was a time when I be - lieved that

your heart sad and blue And so my heart is
you be - longed to me But now I know your

pay - ing now for things I did - n't
heart is shack - led to a mem - o -

do In an - ger, un - kind words are said that
ry The more I learn to care for you the

make the tear - drops start Why can't I free your
more we drift a - part Why can't I free your

doubt - ful mind and melt your Cold, Cold
doubt - ful mind and

Heart? You'll melt your Cold, Cold Heart?

COWBOY TAKE ME AWAY

Words and Music by MARTIE SEIDEL
and MARCUS HUMMON

© 1999 WOOLLY PUDDIN' MUSIC (BMI)/Administered by BUG MUSIC,
CAREERS-BMG MUSIC PUBLISHING, INC. and FLOYD'S DREAM MUSIC
All Rights for FLOYD'S DREAM MUSIC Administered by CAREERS-BMG MUSIC PUBLISHING, INC.
All Rights Reserved   Used by Permission

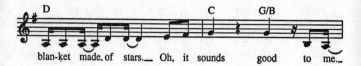

blan-ket made of stars._ Oh, it sounds good to me._

I said, cow-boy, take_ me_ a-way.

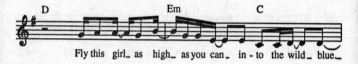

Fly this girl_ as high_ as you can_ in-to the wild_ blue_

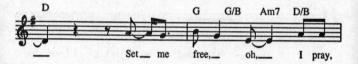

Set_ me free,_ oh,_ I pray,

clos-er_ to heav-en a-bove_ and clos-er to_ you,_

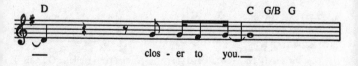

_ clos-er to you._

I wan-na

walk and not run._____ I wan-na

skip and not___ fall._____ I wan-na

look at the___ ho-ri-zon and not see___

___ a build-ing stand-in' tall.___ I wan-na

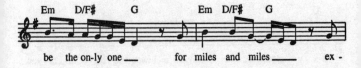

be the on-ly one___ for miles and miles____ ex-

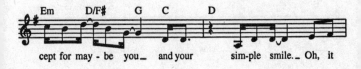

cept for may-be you___ and your sim-ple smile.___ Oh, it

sounds good to me.___ Yes, it sounds___

%
C   G/B   D

_ so good _ to me. _   Cow-boy,

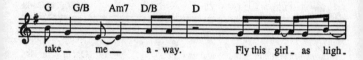

G   G/B   Am7   D/B   D

take _ me _ a - way.   Fly this girl _ as high _

Em   C   D

_ as you can _ in - to the wild _ blue. _   Set _ me

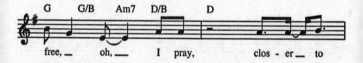

G   G/B   Am7   D/B   D

free, _   oh, _   I   pray,   clos - er _ to

Em   C   D/F#   D   To Coda ⊕

heav-en a - bove _ and clos-er to _ you, _   clos-er to you. _

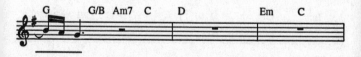

G   G/B Am7   C   D   Em   C

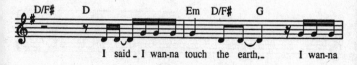

D/F#   D   Em D/F#   G

I said _ I wan-na touch the earth, _   I wan-na

break it in ___ my hands. _____ I wan-na

grow some-thing wild ___ and un - rul - y. Oh, it sounds ___

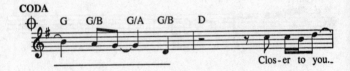

CODA

Clos - er to you. ___

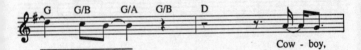

Cow - boy,

take me a - way, ___ clos - er to you. ___

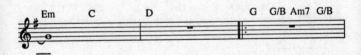

DOES FORT WORTH EVER CROSS YOUR MIND

Words and Music DARLENE SHAFER and SANGER D. SHAFER

Cold Fort Worth beer just ain't no
Dar - lin' while you're bus - y burn - ing

good _____ for jeal - ous.
bridg - es, _____

I try _____ it night _____ af - ter
burn one for _____ me if you get time. _____

night. You're in
_____ 'Cause good mem - o -

some - one el - se's arms _____ in
ries don't fade so eas -

Dal - las. } Does Fort _____ Worth
y. _____ }

Copyright © 1976 by Acuff-Rose Music, Inc.
All Rights Reserved   Used by Permission

ev - er   cross   your   mind?

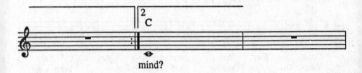

mind?

You   left   me   here ___   to   be   with

him _____   in   Dal - las,   and

I   know   it   hurt ___   you   at   the

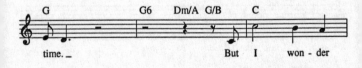

time. ___   But   I   won - der

now ___   if   it   makes ___   a

CRAZY

Words and Music by
WILLIE NELSON

Copyright © 1961 Sony/ATV Songs LLC
Copyright Renewed
All Rights Administered by Sony/ATV Music Publishing, 8 Music Square West, Nashville, TN 37203
International Copyright Secured   All Rights Reserved

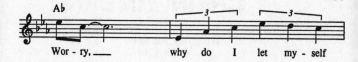

Ab

Wor - ry, _____ why do I let my - self

Eb   F7

wor - ry; _____   Won - d'rin' ___

Bb7   Bb7#5

what in the world did I do.

Eb   C7

Cra - zy _____   for think - ing that my love could

Fm

hold you, _____   I'm

Ab   Gm   Fm   Cm

Cra - zy for try - in',   Cra - zy for cry - in' and I'm

Fm7   Bb7   Eb

Cra - zy for lov - in' you.

CRYIN' TIME

Words and Music by
BUCK OWENS

Oh, it's Cry-in' Time a-gain, ___ you're gon-na leave me; I can see that far a-way look in your eye. I can tell by the way you held me, dar-ling, ___ that it won't be long be-fore it's Cry-in' Time.

{ 1. Now they say that ab-sence makes the heart grow
{ 2. *(See additional lyrics)*

Copyright © 1964 Sony/ATV Songs LLC, Beachaven Music Corp. and Jarest Music Company
Copyright Renewed
All Rights on behalf of Sony/ATV Songs LLC Administered by
Sony/ATV Music Publishing, 8 Music Square West, Nashville, TN 37203
International Copyright Secured   All Rights Reserved

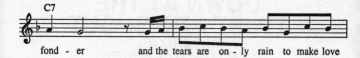

fond - er and the tears are on - ly rain to make love

grow, well, my love for you could nev - er grow no

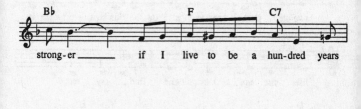

strong - er _____ if I live to be a hun - dred years

old. Oh, it's old. Oh, it's

Additional Lyrics

2. Now, you say that you've found someone you loved better;
That's the way it's happened every time before.
And as sure as the sun comes up tomorrow
Cryin' Time will start when you walk out the door.
(Chorus)

DOWN AT THE TWIST AND SHOUT

Words and Music by
MARY CHAPIN CARPENTER

Fast Country two–beat

Sat-ur-day night and the moon is out. I wan-na head on o - ver to the Twist and Shout, find a two-step part - ner and a Ca - jun beat, when it lifts me up, I'm gon-na find my feet out in the mid-dle of a big dance floor. When I hear that fid - dle, wan-na beg for more. Wan-na dance to a band from a - Loui-si-an' to - night.

© 1990 EMI APRIL MUSIC INC. and GETAREALJOB MUSIC
All Rights Controlled and Administered by EMI APRIL MUSIC INC.
All Rights Reserved   International Copyright Secured   Used by Permission

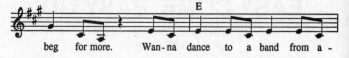

beg for more. Wan-na dance to a band from a-

Loui-si-an'___ to-night. Hey!

(Whoo!)

(Instrumental)

To Coda ⊕   D.S. al Coda

They got a   Bring your

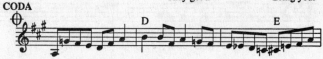

CODA
⊕

EASY COME, EASY GO

**Words and Music by DEAN DILLON
and AARON BARKER**

Moderately, relaxed

She says she's had e - nough of me.
We tried to work it out a hun-dred times;

I've had e - nough of her, ___ too.
nine - ty - nine it did - n't work.

I might as well go on and set her free; ___
I think it's best we put it all be - hind ___

she's al - read - y turned me loose.
be-fore we wind up get - tin' hurt.

No fault, no blame, no-bod - y done no wrong;
No hard feel-in's, dar-lin', no re - grets;

that's just the way it some - times goes.
no tears ___ and no bro-ken hearts.

Copyright © 1992 by Acuff-Rose Music, Inc. and O-Tex Music
All Rights Reserved Used Permission

74

CODA

go.
(Vocal ad lib. on repeat)

Eas - y come, __ girl, eas - y __

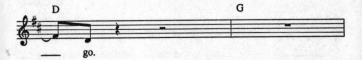

__ go.

Vay - a con Di - os, good luck!

FOOLISH PRIDE

Words and Music by
TRAVIS TRITT

She stayed up all night and cried into her pil-
re-lives ev-'ry word they spoke in ang-

-low, and fought off the urge to just
-er, He walks the floor and punch-

break down and call. Last
-es out the wall. To

night to find the fault seemed so darned eas-y,
a-pol-o-gize to her would be so sim-ple,

but now, who's to blame don't mat-ter much at all.
but in-stead he cries, "I'll be damned if I'll crawl."

She thinks, if she calls him,
If he los-es her,

Copyright © 1994 Post Oak Publishing, Inc.
International Copyright Secured   All Rights Reserved

FOR THE GOOD TIMES

Words and Music by
KRIS KRISTOFFERSON

Copyright © 1968 by Careers-BMG Music Publishing, Inc.
Copyright Renewed
International Copyright Secured   All Rights Reserved

FOREVER'S AS FAR AS I'LL GO

Words and Music by
MIKE REID

Copyright © 1990 ALMO MUSIC CORP. and BRIO BLUES MUSIC
All Rights Administered by ALMO MUSIC CORP.
All Rights Reserved Used by Permission

82

Ab(add2) ... Ab/Bb

ev - er's __ as far __ as __ I __

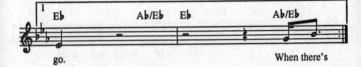

1 Eb ... Ab/Eb Eb ... Ab/Eb

go. ... When there's

2 Eb ... Eb/G Ab(add2)

go. ... for - ev - er's __ as far __

Ab/Bb Bb Ab/Bb Bb

as

Ab(add2) ... Gm

I'll go. *(Instrumental)*

Cm ... Ab(add2)

Repeat ad lib. and Fade

Gm ... Cm ... Ab(add2)

HARD ROCK BOTTOM
OF YOUR HEART

Words and Music by
HUGH PRESTWOOD

Copyright © 1989 by Careers-BMG Music Publishing, Inc. and Hugh Prestwood Music
All Rights Administered by Careers-BMG Music Publishing, Inc.
International Copyright Secured   All Rights Reserved

FRIENDS IN LOW PLACES

Words and Music by DEWAYNE BLACKWELL
and EARL BUD LEE

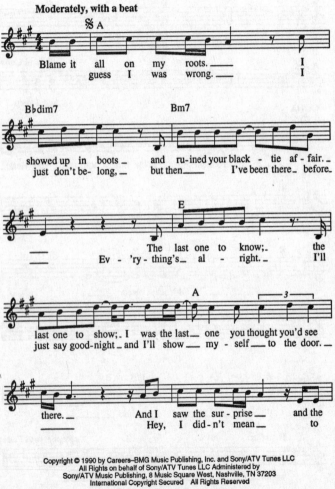

Copyright © 1990 by Careers–BMG Music Publishing, Inc. and Sony/ATV Tunes LLC
All Rights on behalf of Sony/ATV Tunes LLC Administered by
Sony/ATV Music Publishing, 8 Music Square West, Nashville, TN 37203
International Copyright Secured   All Rights Reserved

88

I'm not big___ on so-cial grac- es. Think I'll

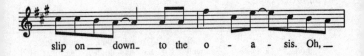

slip on___ down___ to the o-a-sis. Oh,___

Bm7   E   A   To Coda

I've got Friends___ In Low___ Plac - es.___

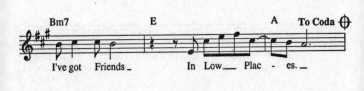

(Instrumental)

Bm7

E   A   D.S. al Coda

Well, I

CODA

I've got Friends___ In

Low Plac - es where the whis-key __ drowns __ and the

beer __ chas - es my blues __ a - way

and I'll be o - kay. ____

Yeah, I'm not big __ on

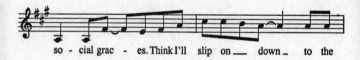

so - cial grac - es. Think I'll slip on __ down __ to the

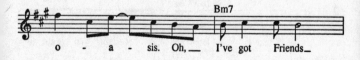

o - a - sis. Oh, __ I've got Friends __

Repeat and Fade

In Low __ Plac - es. __

THE GAMBLER

Words and Music by
DON SCHLITZ

1. On a warm summer's evening on a train bound for nowhere, I met up with a gambler. We were both too tired to sleep. So we took turns a-starin' out the window at the darkness till boredom over took us and he began to speak. He said give you some advice."

2. "Son I've made a life out of readin' people's faces and knowin' what their cards were by the way they held their eyes. So if you don't mind my sayin' I can see you're out of aces; for a taste of your whiskey I'll

3. - 5. (See additional lyrics)

3. So I learn to play it right." "You've got to

know when to hold 'em, know when to fold 'em.

Copyright © 1977 Sony/ATV Tunes LLC
All Rights Administered by Sony/ATV Music Publishing, 8 Music Square West, Nashville, TN 37203
International Copyright Secured   All Rights Reserved

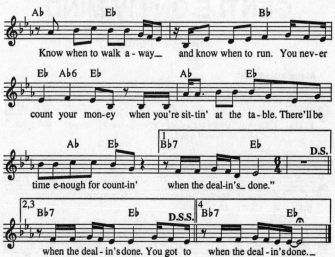

Know when to walk a-way__ and know when to run. You nev-er count your mon-ey when you're sit-tin' at the ta-ble. There'll be time e-nough for count-in' when the deal-in's_ done." when the deal-in's done. You got to when the deal-in's done.__

Additional Lyrics

3. (So I) handed him my bottle,
   And he drank down my last swallow.
   Then he bummed a cigarette and
   Asked me for a light.
   And the night got deathly quiet and
   His face lost all expression.
   Said, "If you're gonna play the game,
   Boy, you gotta learn to play it right."
   (CHORUS)

4. "Ev'ry gambler knows that the secret to survivin'
   Is knowin' when to throw away, and
   Knowin' what to keep.
   'Cause ev'ry hand's a winner, and
   Ev'ry hand's a loser.
   And the best that you can hope for
   Is to die in your sleep." And...

5. When he'd finished speakin'
   He turned back toward the window.
   Crushed out his cigarette and
   Faded off to sleep.
   And somewhere in the darkness
   The Gambler he broke even.
   But in his final words I found
   An ace that I could keep.
   (CHORUS)

GENTLE ON MY MIND

Words and Music by
JOHN HARTFORD

Moderately bright

1. It's know-ing that your door is al-ways o-pen and your
2.-4. *(See additional lyrics)*

path is free to walk,

That makes me tend to leave my sleep-ing

bag rolled up and stashed be-hind your couch,

And it's know-ing I'm not

shack-led by for-got-ten words and bonds___ And the

ink stains that have dried up-on some line,

Copyright © 1967, 1968 (Renewed 1995, 1996) by Ensign Music Corporation
International Copyright Secured   All Rights Reserved

That keeps you in the back-roads by the ri-vers of my mem-'ry that keeps you ev-er Gen-tle On My Mind.

It's

Mind.

Additional Lyrics

2. It's not clinging to the rocks and ivy planted on their columns now that binds me
   Or something that somebody said because they thought we fit together walkin'.
   It's just knowing that the world will not be cursing or forgiving when I walk along
   Some railroad track and find
   That you're moving on the backroads by the rivers of my memory and for hours
   You're just Gentle On My Mind.

3. Though the wheat fields and the clothes lines and junkyards and the highways
   Come between us
   And some other woman crying to her mother 'cause she turned and I was gone.
   I still run in silence, tears of joy might stain my face and summer sun might
   Burn me 'til I'm blind
   But not to where I cannot see you walkin' on the backroads by the rivers flowing
   Gentle On My Mind.

4. I dip my cup of soup back from the gurglin' cracklin' cauldron in some train yard
   My beard a roughning coal pile and a dirty hat pulled low across my face.
   Through cupped hands 'round a tin can I pretend I hold you to my breast and find
   That you're waving from the backroads by the rivers of my memory ever smilin'
   Ever Gentle On My Mind.

GIVE ME WINGS

Words and Music by RHONDA KYE FLEMING
and DON SCHLITZ

Moderately, in 2

He asked her, "What gifts can I bring
He walked o-ver to the

___ you to prove that my
win-dow. He si-lent-ly

love for you __ is true? ___ I
stared in-to space. ___ He

want to make __ you mine ___ for-ev
said, "I just want to pro

-er. ___ There's noth-ing on __ this earth
-tect you, ___ 'cause this world is a

___ I would-n't do." ___ She said,
dan-ger-ous place." She

Copyright © 1986 IRVING MUSIC, INC., EAGLEWOOD MUSIC, UNIVERSAL -
MCA MUSIC PUBLISHING, A Division of UNIVERSAL STUDIOS, INC. and DON SCHLITZ MUSIC
All Rights for EAGLEWOOD MUSIC Controlled and Administered by IRVING MUSIC, INC.
All Rights for DON SCHLITZ MUSIC Controlled and Administered by UNIVERSAL -
MCA MUSIC PUBLISHING, A Division of UNIVERSAL STUDIOS, INC.
All Rights Reserved   Used by Permission

bird in a cage __ will for - get how to sing. __

To Coda ⊕

__ {1., D.S. If you love __ me, give me wings."
You can trust __ me.

Give me wings." __

She said, "Up a - bove __ the clouds __

you can see for - ev - er. And

I know you __ and I __ can learn to fly __

Am   G/B   C   Dsus

to - geth - er. ___

D   **D.S. al Coda**   **CODA**   D7sus   Em G/D

If you love ___   give me wings.___

C   G/B   Am7

If   you   real - ly   love _____   me, ___

D7sus   D

give me   wings.___

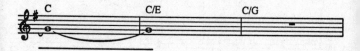

C   C/E   C/G

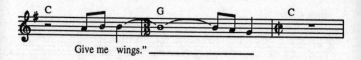

C   G   C

Give me wings." _____

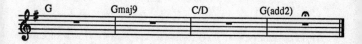

G   Gmaj9   C/D   G(add2)

A GOOD HEARTED WOMAN

Words and Music by WILLIE NELSON and WAYLON JENNINGS

© 1971 (Renewed 1999) FULL NELSON MUSIC, INC. and BARON MUSIC PUBLISHING
All Rights for FULL NELSON MUSIC, INC. Controlled and Administered by EMI LONGITUDE MUSIC
All Rights Reserved International Copyright Secured Used by Permission

F

day; ___
gain. ___

But she nev - er com -
Lord knows she don't un - der -

plains of the bad times or ___
stand him, but she does the ___

F7   Bb

bad things ___ he's done, Lord.
best that ___ she can. ___

She just
'Cause she's a

C7

talks a - bout the good times they've
good - heart - ed wom - an;

had and all the good times to ___
she loves her good - tim - in' ___

F

come. }
man. }
She's   a

good - heart - ed   wom - an ____ in

F7

love   with   a   good - tim - in'

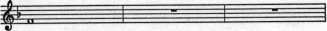

Bb

man.

C7

She   loves   him   in

spite   of   his   ways   that   she

F

don't   un - der - stand.

GREEN GREEN GRASS
OF HOME

Words and Music by
CURLY PUTMAN

Slowly

1. The old home town looks the

2., 3. *(See additional lyrics)*

same ____ as I step down from the

train, And there to meet me is my

Ma - ma and Pa - pa;

And down the road I look and

there runs Ma - ry, hair of gold and

lips like cher - ries. It's good to touch the

Copyright © 1965 Sony/ATV Songs LLC
Copyright Renewed
All Rights Administered by Sony/ATV Music Publishing, 8 Music Square West, Nashville, TN 37203
International Copyright Secured   All Rights Reserved

Green Green Grass Of Home. Yes, they'll all come to meet me, arms a- reach - ing, smil - ing sweet - ly. It's good to touch the Green Green Grass Of Home. Home.

Additional Lyrics

2. The old house is still standing tho' the paint is cracked and dry,
   And there's that old oak tree that I used to play on.
   Down the lane I walk with my sweet Mary, hair of gold and lips like cherries:
   It's good to touch the Green Green Grass Of Home.
   Chorus:

3. Then I awake and look around me at the grey walls that surround me,
   And I realize that I was only dreaming.
   For there's a guard and there's a sad old Padre, arm in arm
   we'll walk at daybreak,
   Again I'll touch the Green Green Grass Of Home.

   Chorus:
   Yes, they'll all come to see me in the shade of that old oak tree,
   As they lay me 'neath the Green Green Grass Of Home.

HAVE MERCY

Words and Music by
PAUL KENNERLEY

Country Rock

D | G

I was stand-ing in line ___ at the cit-y bus stop,

D | A

soaked to the skin from ev-'ry rain-drop. I

D | G

see you driv-ing by just like a phan-tom jet ___ with your

D | A7 | D

arm a-round ___ some lit-tle bru-nette. You

D | G

say you won't be home be-cause you're work-ing late. ___ Hon-ey,
called ___ you up ___ on the ___ tel-e-phone. ___ I could
went ___ to the bank ___ with my lit-tle check-book. The

D | A

I'm no fool, you've been out on a date. ___ The
hear you was play-in' "Hag-gard" and "Jones." ___ I
cash-ier, he gave me the strang-est look. ___ He said, "You

Copyright © 1985 RONDOR MUSIC (LONDON) LTD.
All Rights Administered by IRVING MUSIC, INC.
All Rights Reserved   Used by Permission

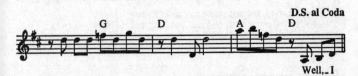

D.S. al Coda

Well,_ I

CODA

mer - cy on me. Have mer - cy___

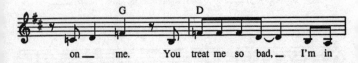

on __ me. You treat me so bad, __ I'm in

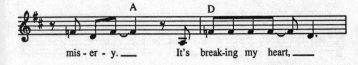

mis - er - y. ___ It's break-ing my heart, ____

Repeat and Fade

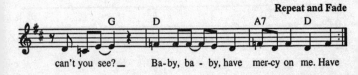

can't you see? _ Ba - by, ba - by, have mer - cy on me. Have

HE DIDN'T HAVE TO BE

Words and Music by KELLEY LOVELACE
and BRAD PAISLEY

When a sin-gle mom_ goes out on a date with some-bod-y new, it al--ways winds_ up feel-in' more like a job in-ter-view. My ma--ma used_ to won-der if_ she'd ev-er meet_ some-one_ that would-n't

© 1999 EMI APRIL MUSIC INC., LOVE RANCH MUSIC and SEA GAYLE MUSIC
All Rights Controlled and Administered by EMI APRIL MUSIC INC.
All Rights Reserved   International Copyright Secured   Used by Permission

find out ___ a - bout ___ me and ___ then

turn a - round ___ and run. ___

I met the man ___ I call ___
met the girl ___ that's now ___

___ my dad ___ when I ___ was five ___ years old.
___ my wife ___ a - bout ___ three years ___ a - go.

___ He took my mom ___ out to ___ a mov -
___ We had ___ the per - fect mar -

- ie and for once ___ I got to go. ___
- riage, but we want - ed some - thin' more.

___ A few ___ months lat - er I ___
___ Now ___ here I stand sur - round -

110

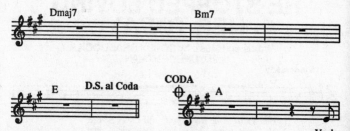

Yeah,

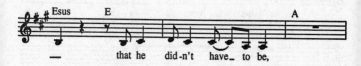

I hope I'm at least___ half the dad___

that he did-n't have___ to be,

be-cause he did-n't have to be,___

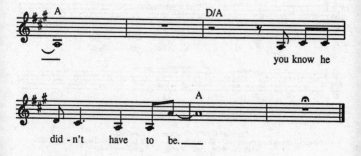

you know he

did-n't have to be.___

HE STOPPED LOVING HER TODAY

Words and Music by BOBBY BRADDOCK
and CURLY PUTMAN

Moderately

G

1. He said, "I'll love you 'til I die,"
2. He kept some let - ters by his bed,

C

She told him, "You'll for - get in time."
dat - ed nine - teen - six - ty - two;

D7

As the years went slow - ly by,
He had un - der - lined in red

G

she still preyed up - on his mind;
ev - ery sin - gle "I love you";

He kept her pic - ture on his wall
I went to see him just to - day,
3. *(See additional lyrics)*

C

and went half - cra - zy now and then;
but I did - n't see no tears;

D7

But he still loved her through it all,
All dressed up to go a - way;

Copyright © 1978, 1980 Sony/ATV Songs LLC
All Rights Administered by Sony/ATV Music Publishing, 8 Music Square West, Nashville, TN 37203
International Copyright Secured   All Rights Reserved

1 hop - ing she'd come __ back a - gain.

2,3 First time I'd seen him smile in years. __

Chorus
He Stopped Lov-ing Her __ To - day;

They placed a wreath. up - on his door; __

And soon they'll car - ry him a - way; __

To Coda

He Stopped Lov - ing Her To - day. __

D.S. al Coda
(3rd ending)

CODA

Additional Lyrics
(Recite)
3. She came to see him one last time
   We all wondered if she would
   And it kept running through my mind
   This time he's over her for good.
   (Chorus)

HE THINKS HE'LL KEEP HER

Words and Music by MARY CHAPIN CARPENTER
and DON SCHLITZ

Moderately fast Rock

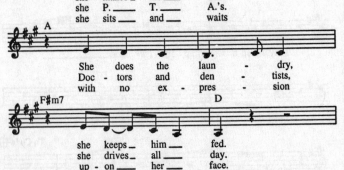

She makes his cof - fee, she makes his bed.
She does the car - pool, she P. T. A.'s.
She packs his suit - case, she sits and waits

She does the laun - dry, she keeps him fed.
Doc - tors and den - tists, she drives all day.
with no ex - pres - sion up - on her face.

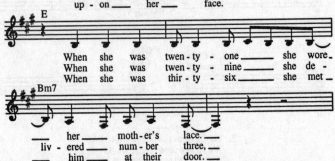

When she was twen - ty - one she wore her moth - er's lace.
When she was twen - ty - nine she de - liv - ered num - ber three,
When she was thir - ty - six she met him at their door.

© 1992 EMI APRIL MUSIC INC., GETAREALJOB MUSIC, BMG SONGS, INC. and NEW DON SONGS
All Rights for GETAREALJOB MUSIC Controlled and Administered by EMI APRIL MUSIC INC.
All Rights Reserved   International Copyright Secured   Used by Permission

She said, "For - ev - er" with ___ a
and ev - 'ry Christ-mas card showed a
She said, "I'm sor - ry, I ___ don't

smile up - on ___ her face. ___
per - fect fam - i - ly. ___
love you an - y - more." ___

Ev - 'ry - thing ___

___ runs right on time, ___ years of prac -

- tice and de - sign. ___ Spit and pol -

- ish till it shines. ___ He thinks he'll

keep ___ her. Ev - 'ry - thing ___

116

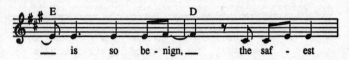

is so be - nign, ___ the saf - est

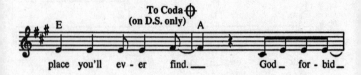

place you'll ev - er find. ___ God ___ for - bid ___

___ you'd change ___ your mind. ___ He thinks he'll

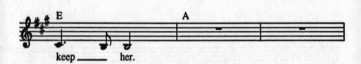

keep ___ her.

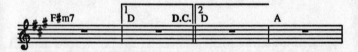

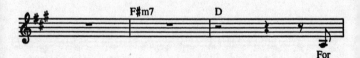

For

fif - teen years ___ she had a job ___ and not ___

Bm7

one raise in pay.

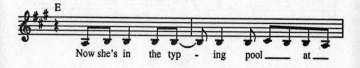

E

Now she's in the typ - ing pool at

F#m **D** **E** **D.S. al Coda**

min - i - mum wage.

CODA

A

At least un - til

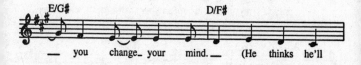

E/G# **D/F#**

you change your mind. (He thinks he'll

E **A**

keep her.)

F#m7 | **1-3 D** | **4 D E A**

HERE YOU COME AGAIN

Words by CYNTHIA WEIL
Music by BARRY MANN

Moderately

Here You Come A - gain, ___
Here You Come A - gain, ___

just when I've ___ be - gun to get my-self to - geth - er, you
just when I'm ___ a - bout to make it work with - out you, you

waltz right in the door, ___ just like you've done be - fore ___ and
look in - to my eyes ___ and lie those pret - ty lies ___ and

1.
wrap ___ my heart ___ 'round your lit - tle fin - ger.

2.
pret - ty soon ___ I'm wond - 'rin ___ how I came to doubt you.

All you got - ta do ___ is smile that smile ___ and

© 1977 SCREEN GEMS-EMI MUSIC INC. and SUMMERHILL SONGS INC.
All Rights Controlled and Administered by SCREEN GEMS-EMI MUSIC INC.
All Rights Reserved   International Copyright Secured   Used by Permission

120

HERE'S A QUARTER
(Call Someone Who Cares)

Words and Music by
TRAVIS TRITT

Copyright © 1991 Sony/ATV Songs LLC and Post Oak Publishing
All Rights Administered by Sony/ATV Music Publishing, 8 Music Square West, Nashville, TN 37203
International Copyright Secured   All Rights Reserved

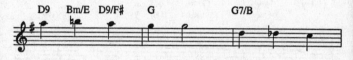

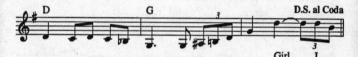

Girl, ___ I ___

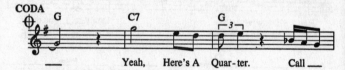

___ Yeah, Here's A Quar-ter. Call ___

some - one ___ who cares. _____

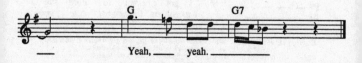

___ Yeah, ___ yeah. _____

HEY, GOOD LOOKIN'

Words and Music by
HANK WILLIAMS

Copyright © 1951 (Renewed 1975) by Acuff-Rose Music, Inc. and Hiriam Music in the U.S.A.
All Rights for Hiriam Music Administered by Rightsong Music Inc.
All Rights outside the U.S.A. Controlled by Acuff-Rose Music, Inc.
All Rights Reserved   Used by Permission

HONKY TONK BLUES

Words and Music by
HANK WILLIAMS

Moderately slow

F7

I left my home_down on a ru-ral route_ And
I stopped in-to ev-'ry place in town_ This
tuck my wor-ries un-der-neath my arm_ And

told my folks_ I'm go-in' step-pin' out_ to get the
cit-y life_ has real-ly got me down_ I got the
get right back to my Pap-py's farm_ and leave the

Bb7

Honk-y Tonk Blues _____ The jump-in'
Honk-y Tonk Blues _____ I got the
Honk-y Tonk Blues _____ For-get the

F7

Honk-y Tonk Blues _____
Honk-y Tonk Blues _____
Honk-y Tonk Blues _____ I don't

C7

Lord, I got 'em _____ I got the
Lord, I'm suf-ferin' _____ with the
want to be both-ered _____ with the

F7

Honk - y Tonk Blues
Honk - y Tonk Blues When

Copyright © 1948 (Renewed 1975) by Acuff-Rose Music, Inc. and Hiriam Music in the U.S.A.
All Rights for Hiriam Music Administered by Rightsong Music Inc.
All Rights outside the U.S.A. Controlled by Acuff-Rose Music, Inc.
All Rights Reserved Used by Permission

I went to ___ a dance, wore out my shoes, ___ Woke
I get home ___ a - gain to Ma and Pa, ___ I

up this morn - in' wish - in' I could lose ___ the jump - in'
know they're gon - na lay down down the law ___ a - bout the

Bb7

Honk - y Tonk Blues _____ The wea - ry
Honk - y Tonk Blues _____ The jump - in'

F7

Honk - y Tonk Blues _____
Honk - y Tonk Blues _____

C7

Lord I'm suf - ferin' _____ with the
Lord I'm suf - ferin' _____ with the

1,2 F

Honk - y Tonk Blues.
Honk - y Tonk Blues. Gon - na

3 F

Honk - y Tonk Blues.

HONKY TONKIN'

Words and Music by
HANK WILLIAMS

Copyright © 1948 (Renewed 1975) by Acuff-Rose Music, Inc. and Hiriam Music in the U.S.A.
All Rights for Hiriam Music Administered by Rightsong Music Inc.
All Rights outside the U.S.A. Controlled by Acuff-Rose Music, Inc.
All Rights Reserved Used by Permission

I CAN LOVE YOU LIKE THAT

Words and Music by MARIBETH DERRY, JENNIFER KIMBALL and STEVE DIAMOND

Moderate Ballad

They read you Cin-der-el-la, you hoped it would come true that
nev-er make a prom-ise I don't in-tend to keep. So,

one day your Prince Charm-ing would come _ res-cue you. _ You
when I say for-ev-er, for-ev-er's what I mean.

like ro-man-tic mov-ies; you nev-er will _ for-get the
I'm no Ca-sa-no-va, but I swear this much is true:

way you felt when Ro-me-o kissed Ju-li-et. _ You
I'll be hold-ing noth-ing back when it comes to you. You

All this time that you've been wait - ing,
dream of love that's ev-er-last-ing. Well,

Copyright © 1995 Criterion Music Corp., EMI Full Keel Music Co.,
Friends And Angels Music, Second Wave Music and Diamond Cuts
All Rights for Friends And Angels Music Controlled and Administered by EMI Full Keel Music Co.
All Rights for Second Wave Music Administered by
Universal-MCA Music Publishing, A Division of Universal Studios, Inc.
All Rights for Diamond Cuts Administered by Zomba Enterprises, Inc.
All Rights Reserved   Used by Permission

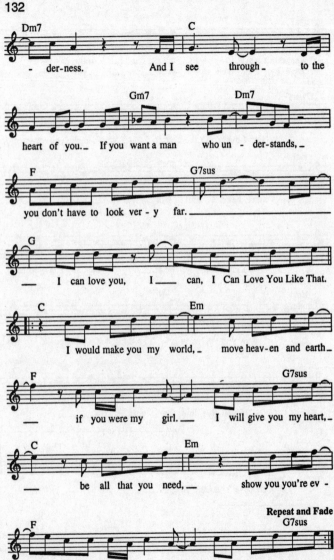

I WALK THE LINE

Words and Music by
JOHN R. CASH

Moderately bright

1. I keep a close watch on this heart of mine. ___ I keep my eyes wide o - pen all the time. ___ I keep the ends out for the tie that binds. Be - cause you're mine ___ I walk the line. ___ I find it line. ___

2. ver - y ver - y eas - y to be true. ___ I find my - self a - lone when each day is through. ___ Yes, I'll ad - mit that I'm a fool for you. Be - cause you're mine ___ I walk the line. ___ As sure as line. ___

3.-5. *(See additional lyrics)*

Additional Lyrics

3. As sure as night is dark and day is light,
   I keep you on my mind both day and night.
   And happiness I've known proves that it's right.
   Because you're mine I walk the line.

4. You've got a way to keep me on your side.
   You give me cause for love that I can't hide.
   For you I know I'd even try to turn the tide.
   Because you're mine I walk the line.

5. I keep a close watch on this heart of mine.
   I keep my eyes wide open all the time.
   I keep the ends out for the tie that binds.
   Because you're mine I walk the line.

© 1956 (Renewed 1984) HOUSE OF CASH, INC. (BMI)/Administered by BUG MUSIC
All Rights Reserved   Used by Permission

I CAN'T STOP LOVING YOU

Words and Music by
DON GIBSON

Slowly

Those hap-py hours _____ that we once knew, _____ though long a - go, _____ still make me blue. _____ They say that time _____ heals _____ a bro - ken heart, _____ but time has stood still _____ since we've been a - part. _____ { I can't stop
{ I can't stop

Copyright © 1958 (Renewed 1985) by Acuff-Rose Music, Inc.
All Rights Reserved   Used by Permission

I FALL TO PIECES

Words and Music by HANK COCHRAN
and HARLAN HOWARD

Copyright © 1960 Sony/ATV Songs LLC
Copyright Renewed
International Copyright Secured   All Rights Reserved

You want me to act like we've
You tell me to act find some - one

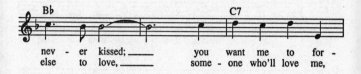

nev - er kissed; _____ you want me to for -
else to love, _____ some - one who'll love me,

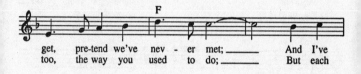

get, pre-tend we've nev - er met; _____ And I've
too, the way you used to do; _____ But each

tried _____ and I've tried, but I have - n't yet; _____
time _____ I go out with _ some - one new;

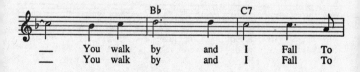

_ You walk by and I Fall To
_ You walk by and I Fall To

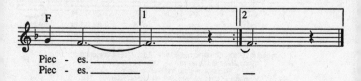

Piec - es. _____
Piec - es. _____

I HOPE YOU DANCE

Words and Music by TIA SILLERS
and MARK D. SANDERS

Copyright © 2000 by Choice Is Tragic Music, Ensign Music Corporation,
Soda Creek and Universal - MCA Music Publishing,
A Division of Universal Studios, Inc.
International Copyright Secured   All Rights Reserved

— you emp - ty hand - ed.
— but it's ___ worth mak - in'.

Eb **F**

(1., D.S.) I hope you still ___ feel small _ when you
(2.) Don't let ___ some hell - bent ___

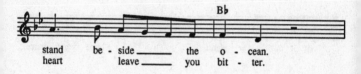

Bb

stand be - side ___ the o - cean.
heart leave ___ you bit - ter.

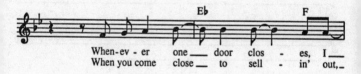

Eb **F**

When-ev - er one ___ door clos - es, I ___
When you come close ___ to sell - in' out, ___

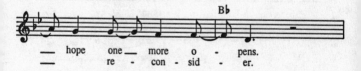

Bb

— hope one ___ more o - pens.
— re - con - sid - er.

Cm7 **Bb/D**

Prom - ise me ___ that you'll _ give faith _
Give the heav - ens a - bove more _

_____ a fight - ing chance.
_____ than just a pass - ing glance.

And when you get the choice to

To Coda
Fsus F

sit it out or dance, I hope you dance.

1
Gm   Eb   Bb   F/A

Gm   Eb

I hope _ you dance. _____

Fsus   F

I hope _ you

2

Gm   E♭

(Time   is   a   wheel   in   con - stant

B♭   F/A

mo - tion,   al - ways   roll -

I   hope __ you

Gm   E♭

- ing   us ____ a - long.) __

dance. _____

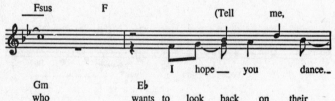

Fsus   F

(Tell   me,

I   hope __ you   dance..

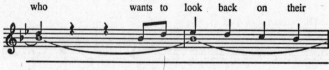

Gm   E♭

who   wants to   look   back   on   their

B♭   F/A

youth   and   won - der   where __

I   hope __ you

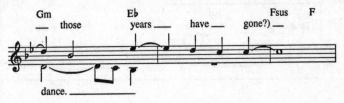

those years have gone?) dance.

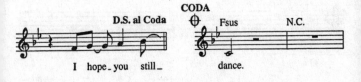

D.S. al Coda

CODA

I hope you still dance.

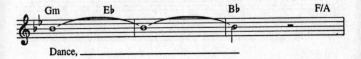

Dance,

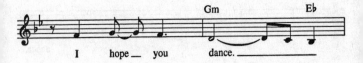

I hope you dance.

I hope you dance.

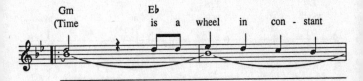

(Time is a wheel in con - stant

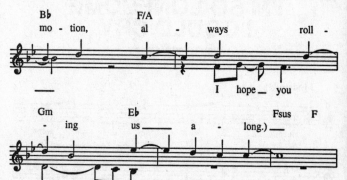

Bb   **F/A**

mo - tion,   al - ways   roll -

I hope___ you

Gm   **Eb**   **Fsus**   **F**

- ing   us ___ a - long.) ___

dance. ___

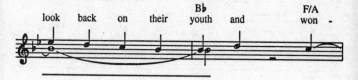

(Tell   me,   who   **Gm**   wants to   **Eb**

I hope___ you   dance. ___

look   back   on   their   **Bb** youth   and   **F/A** won -

- der   where ___ those   **Gm**   years ___ **Eb**

I hope___ you   dance. ___

have ___ gone?) ___ **Fsus**   **F**

Repeat and Fade

I hope___ you   dance. ___

I'M SO LONESOME I COULD CRY

Words and Music by
HANK WILLIAMS

Copyright © 1949 (Renewed 1976) by Acuff-Rose Music, Inc. and Hiriam Music in the U.S.A.
All Rights for Hiriam Music Administered by Rightsong Music Inc,
All Rights outside the U.S.A. Controlled by Acuff-Rose Music, Inc.
All Rights Reserved   Used by Permission

IF YOU CHANGE
YOUR MIND

Words and Music by HANK DeVITO
and ROSANNE CASH

Moderately fast

If ___ you change ___ your mind
When ___ the time ___ is right,

and leave ___ the past ___ be - hind,
I ___ can hold ___ you tight.

you ___ know where ___ you'll al - ways
You ___ know I can wait ___ for -

find me. ___ And if ___ she
ev - er. ___ And time ___ is

breaks ___ your heart and tears ___ your
on ___ our side and we ___ can

world ___ a - part, you ___ can al -
sure - ly find all ___ the love ___

Copyright © 1987 ALMO MUSIC CORP., LITTLE NEMO MUSIC and CHELCATE MUSIC
All Rights for LITTLE NEMO MUSIC Controlled and Administered by ALMO MUSIC CORP.
All Rights Reserved   Used by Permission

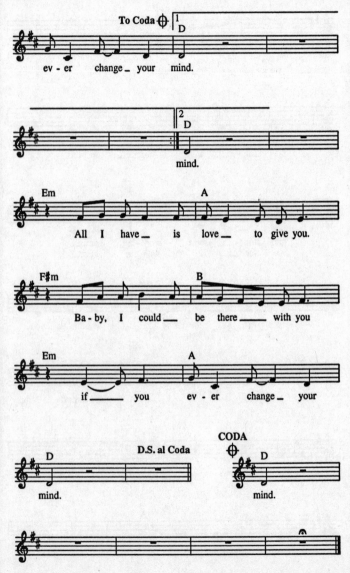

ev - er change your mind.

mind.

All I have is love to give you.

Ba - by, I could be there with you

if you ev - er change your

mind.

mind.

JUST ANOTHER DAY IN PARADISE

Words and Music by PHIL VASSAR
and CRAIG WISEMAN

The kids scream-in', the phone ring-in',
Fri - day, __ you're late. __

and dog bark-in' at the mail - man bring-in' that
I guess we'll nev - er make our din-ner date ____ at the

stack of bills, o - ver-due.
res - tau - rant. You start to cry.

Good morn-in', ba - by, how are you? Got - ta
Ba - by, we'll __ just __ im-pro-vise. Well,

half hour, a quick show - er.
Plan B, looks like __

Take a drink of milk, but the milk's gone sour. __ My
Dom - i - no's __ Piz - za in the can-dle-light. __ Then we'll

© 2000 EMI APRIL MUSIC INC., PHIL VASSAR MUSIC and BMG SONGS, INC.
All Rights for PHIL VASSAR MUSIC Controlled and Administered by EMI APRIL MUSIC INC.
All Rights Reserved International Copyright Secured Used by Permission

Bm ... **A**

fun - ny face   makes you laugh.
tip - py - toe   to our room   and

G ... **A**

Twist the top   on   and I   put it back.
make a lit - tle love   that's _ o - ver - due.   But

Bm ... **A**

There goes   the wash - in'   ma - chine. _
some - bod - y   had a   bad   dream. _

G ... **A**

Bm ... **A**

Ba - by, don't   kick   it,   prom - ise   I'll   fix   it
Ma - ma and   Dad - dy, can   me and my   ted - dy

Em7 ... **D/F#** ... **G** ... **A**

long with 'bout a mil - lion oth - er things. _ Well, it's
come _ in and sleep _ in be - tween? _ Yeah, it's

D ... **G**

O   K,   it's   so   nice.

153

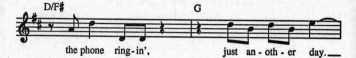

the phone ring-in', just an-oth-er day.

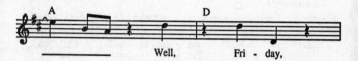

Well, Fri - day,

you're late.

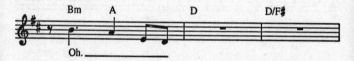

Oh.

It's just an-oth-er day in

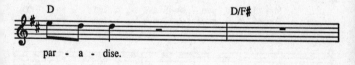

par - a - dise.

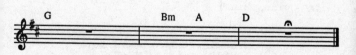

JAMBALAYA
(On the Bayou)

Words and Music by
HANK WILLIAMS

Moderately

1. Good - bye Joe, me got - ta go, me oh
2. daux, Fon - tain - eaux, the place is
3. *(See additional lyrics)*

my oh ___ Me got - ta go pole the
buzz - in' ___ Kin - folk come to see Y -

pi - rogue down the bay - ou ___ My Y -
vonne ___ by the doz - en ___ Dress in

vonne, the sweet - est one, me oh my oh ___
style and go hog wild, me oh my oh ___

Son of a gun, we'll have big fun on the
Son of a gun, we'll have big fun on the

bay - ou ___ }
bay - ou ___ } Jam - ba - la - ya and a craw - fish

Copyright © 1952 (Renewed 1980) by Acuff-Rose Music, Inc. and Hiriam Music in the U.S.A.
All Rights for Hiriam Music Administered by Rightsong Music Inc.
All Rights outside the U.S.A. Controlled by Acuff-Rose Music, Inc.
All Rights Reserved   Used by Permission

pie and fil - let gum - bo _____ 'Cause to -

night I'm gon - na see my ma cher a -

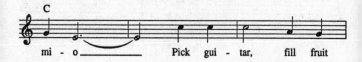

mi - o _____ Pick gui - tar, fill fruit

jar and be gay - o _____ Son of a

gun, we'll have big fun on the bay - ou _____

_____ Thi - bo - bay - ou _____

Additional Lyrics

3. Settle down far from town, get me a pirogue,
   And I'll catch all the fish in the bayou,
   Swap my mon to buy Yvonne what she need-o,
   Son of a gun, we'll have big fun on the bayou.

THE KEEPER
OF THE STARS

**Words and Music by KAREN STALEY,
DANNY MAYO and DICKEY LEE**

Copyright © 1994 by Careers-BMG Music Publishing, Inc., Sixteen Stars Music,
Murrah Music Corporation, Universal-Songs Of PolyGram International, Inc. and Pal Time Music
International Copyright Secured   All Rights Reserved

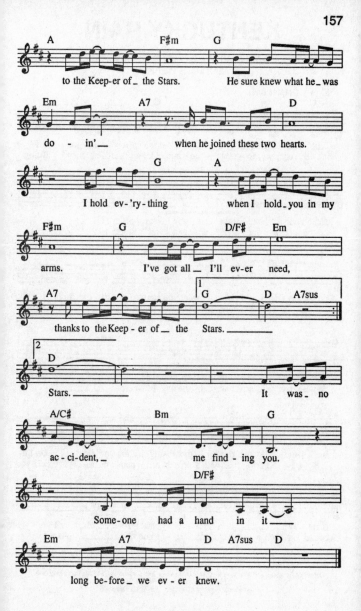

KENTUCKY RAIN

Words and Music by EDDIE RABBITT
and DICK HEARD

Copyright © 1970 by Elvis Presley Music, Inc. and S-P-R Music Corp.
Copyright Renewed and Assigned to Elvis Presley Music and Careers-BMG Music Publishing, Inc.
All Rights Administered by R&H Music
International Copyright Secured   All Rights Reserved

loved you much too long, and my love's too strong, To
drove on thru the rain, as he lis-tened, I ex-plained, And he

let you go, nev-er know-ing what went wrong.
left me with a prayer that I'd find you.

Ken-tuck-y Rain keeps pour-ing down,

And up a-head's an-oth-er town that I'll go

walk-ing thru, With the rain in my shoes,

Search-ing for you,

In the cold Ken-tuck-y Rain,

1.
In the cold Ken-tuck-y Rain.

2.
Rain, In the cold Ken-tuck-y

Repeat and Fade

KING OF THE ROAD

Words and Music by
ROGER MILLER

Copyright © 1964 Sony/ATV Songs LLC
Copyright Renewed
All Rights Administered by Sony/ATV Music Publishing, 8 Music Square West, Nashville, TN 37203
International Copyright Secured   All Rights Reserved

man   of   means   by   no   means

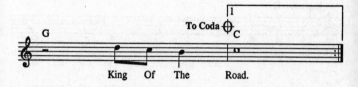

King   Of   The   Road.

Road   I know   ev - er - y   en - gi - neer on

ev - er - y   train   all   of the   chil - dren   and

all of their   names   And   ev - er - y   hand - out   in

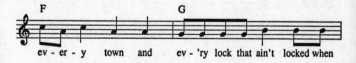

ev - er - y   town   and   ev - 'ry lock that ain't   locked when

no one's a - round. I sing

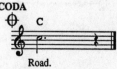

Road.

KISS THIS

Words and Music by AARON TIPPIN,
THEA TIPPIN and PHILLIP DOUGLAS

Moderately

She was a wom-an on a mis-sion, here to
next thing I re-call she had him

drown him and for-get him. So I
back a-gainst the wall,

set her up _____ a-gain to wash him
chew-in' him like a bull-dog on a

down. She had just a-bout suc-ceed-ed when that
bone. She was put-tin' him in his place and I mean

low-down, no-good, cheat-in',
right up in his face,

good for noth-in' came strut-tin' through the
drag-gin' him down a list of done-me-

Copyright © 2000 by Acuff-Rose Music, Inc.,
Thea Later Music, Curb Songs, Charlie Monk Music and Mick Hits
All Rights Reserved   Used by Permission

F

think we're just gonna kiss and make up, don't you?" That's when she said,
and let him have it again, man. She said, she said,

Bb5   C

"Why don't you   kiss,   kiss

this.   And   I

F

don't   mean   on   my   ros - y   red

C

lips.   Me and   you,   ah, we're

through   and   there's

F

on - ly   one   thing   left   for   you   to

do. ___ You ___ just

come on o - ver here one last time.

To Coda ⊕

Puck-er up ___ and close your eyes _____ and kiss

this good - bye."

Well, the this. ___ Hey, kiss

D.S. al Coda

CODA ⊕

this ___ good - bye. Hey, kiss

this good - bye." *(Spoken:) See ya.*

LET ME TELL YOU ABOUT LOVE

Words and Music by BRENT MAHER,
CARL PERKINS and PAUL KENNERLY

Copyright © 1989 Sony/ATV Tunes LLC, Blue Quill Music,
Brick Hithouse Music and Rondor Music (London) Ltd.
All Rights on behalf of Sony/ATV Tunes LLC and Blue Quill Music Administered by
Sony/ATV Music Publishing, 8 Music Square West, Nashville, TN 37203
All Rights on behalf of Rondor Music (London) Ltd. in the USA and Canada Administered by Irving Music, Inc.
International Copyright Secured All Rights Reserved

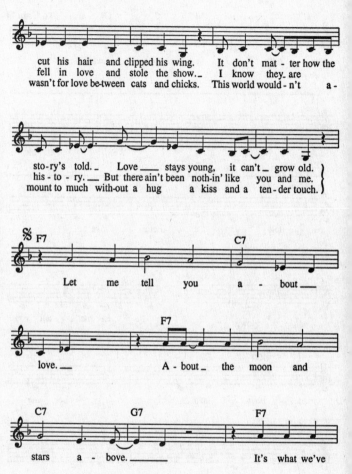

cut his hair and clipped his wing. It don't mat - ter how the
fell in love and stole the show._ I know they_ are
wasn't for love be-tween cats and chicks. This world would - n't a-

sto-ry's told. _ Love ___ stays young, it can't _ grow old.
his - to - ry. _ But there ain't been noth-in' like you and me.
mount to much with-out a hug a kiss and a ten - der touch.

Let me tell you a - bout ___

love. _ A - bout _ the moon and

stars a - bove. ___ It's what we've

all been dream - ing ___ of. ___ Let me

168

LUCILLE

Words and Music by ROGER BOWLING
and HAL BYNUM

In a moderate Country 3

In a bar in To - le - do __ a -
mir - ror I saw him __ and

cross from the de - pot, _____ on a
I close - ly watched him, _____ I __

bar - stool she took off __ her ring.
thought how he looked out __ of place.

I thought I'd __ get clos - er, __ so
He came to __ the wom - an __ who

I walked __ on __ o - ver, I sat down and
sat there __ be - side me, he had a strange

Copyright © 1976 Sony/ATV Songs LLC and Andite Invasion Music
All Rights on behalf of Sony/ATV Songs LLC Administered by
Sony/ATV Music Publishing, 8 Music Square West, Nashville, TN 37203
International Copyright Secured   All Rights Reserved

asked her her name. ___ When the
look on his face. ___ The

drinks fin - 'ly hit ___ her, ___ she said, "I'm ___ no
big hands were cal - loused, ___ he looked like ___ a

quit - ter, ___ but I fin - 'ly quit liv - ing ___ on
moun - tain, ___ for a min - ute I thought I ___ was

dreams. I'm hun - gry for
dead. But he start - ed

laugh - ter and here ev - er - af - ter, ___ I'm
shak - ing, his big heart was break - ing, ___ he

af - ter what-ev - er ___ the oth - er ___ life

brings." In the turned to the

wom-an ___ and said: "You picked a

fine time to leave ___ me, Lu - cille,

with four hun - gry chil - dren and a

crop in the field.

I've had some bad times, ___ lived through some

sad times, ___ but this time ___ your hurt - in' won't

heal, You picked a fine time to

leave me, Lu - cille."

Af - ter he left us ___ I or - dered ___ more ___ whis - key, ___ I must - 've thought I'd lost my mind; ___ I could - n't hold ___ her ___ 'cause the words that he told ___ her ___ kept com - ing ___ back time af - ter time: ___ You picked a

fine time to leave ___ me, Lu - cille,

with four hun - gry chil - dren and a

crop in the field.

I've had some bad times, ___ lived through some

sad times, ___ but this time your hurt - in' won't

heal, you picked a fine time to

leave me, Lu - cille. You picked a

Repeat and Fade

LOVE IS ALIVE

Words and Music by
KENT M. ROBBINS

Slow Country

Love ain't a can - dle.
Love ____ ain't just a moon.

It does-n't burn for one night__ or need the dark to shine__
A dis-tant far a - way dream__ that needs the night to rise.__

Love is a - live.__
Love is a - live.__

And
And

love ____ ain't just a word,__
love ____ ain't just a song,__

in ev-'ry dic - tion-ar - y, but no-where de - fined__
sweet words__ of mu - sic to go danc - in' by.__

Copyright © 1984 IRVING MUSIC, INC.
All Rights Reserved   Used by Permission

Love is a man,_ and he's mine._

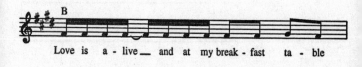

Love is a - live_ and at my break - fast ta - ble

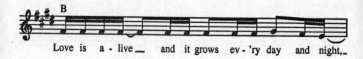

ev - er - y day_ of the week.

Love is a - live_ and it grows ev - 'ry day and night,_

_ e - ven in our sleep._

Love is a - live_ and it's made a hap - py

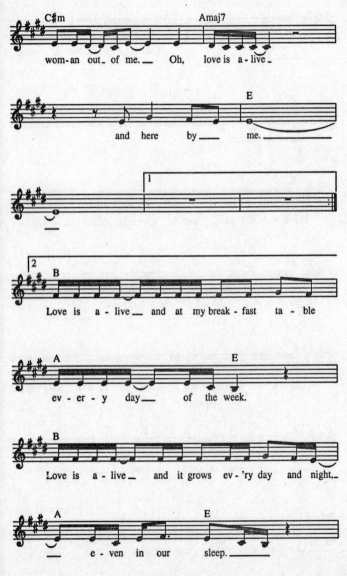

Love is a - live ___ and it's made a hap - py

wom-an out ___ of me. ___ Oh, love is a-live ___

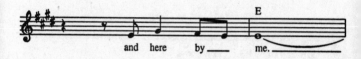

and here by ___ me. ___

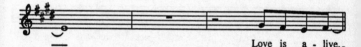

___ Love is a - live, ___

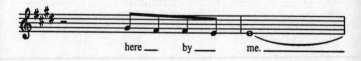

here ___ by ___ me. ___

Repeat and Fade

Love is a - live, ___

MAMMAS DON'T LET YOUR BABIES GROW UP TO BE COWBOYS

Words and Music by ED BRUCE
and PATSY BRUCE

Mam - mas Don't Let Your Ba - bies Grow

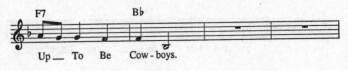

Up __ To Be Cow - boys.

Don't let 'em pick gui - tars and

drive them old trucks. Make 'em be

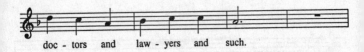

doc - tors and law - yers and such.

Mam - mas __ Don't Let Your Ba - bies Grow

Copyright © 1975 Sony/ATV Songs LLC
All Rights Administered by Sony/ATV Music Publishing, 8 Music Square West, Nashville, TN 37203
International Copyright Secured All Rights Reserved

Up __ To Be Cow - boys,

'Cause they'll nev - er stay __ home, and they're

al - ways a - lone, E - ven with

some - one __ they love.

1. A cow-boy ain't eas - y to
2. *(See additional lyrics)*

love, and he's hard - er __ to hold.

And it means more to him to

give you a song than sil - ver or

gold.

Bud - weis - er buck - les and soft fad - ed

Le - vis' and each night be - gins a new

day. If you can't un - der -

stand _ him _ and he don't die _ young, He'll

prob - a - bly just ride _ a - way.

D.C. al Fine

Additional Lyrics

2. A cowboy loves smokey ole pool rooms and clear mountain mornings,
   Little warm puppies and children and girls of the night.
   Them that don't know him won't like him and them that do sometimes
   won't know how to take him.
   He's not wrong he's just different and his pride won't let him do things
   to make you think he's right.
   Chorus

MY BEST FRIEND

Words and Music by AIMEE MAYO
and BILL LUTHER

Copyright © 1999 by Careers-BMG Music Publishing, Inc.
International Copyright Secured All Rights Reserved

to my life. ___
how much I have. ___

It was a feel - in'
And I still ___ trem - ble

I'd nev - er known. ___
when we touch. ___

And for the first ___ time ___
And, oh, the look ___ in your eyes

I did - n't feel a - lone. ___ }
when we make love. ___ }
You're

more _____ than a lov - er.

There could nev - er be an - oth - er

to make me feel the way ___ you do.

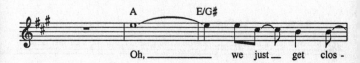

Oh, _____ we just ___ get clos -

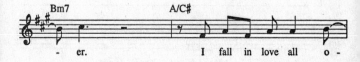

- er. I fall in love all o -

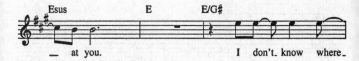

- ver ev - 'ry time I look _

_ at you. I don't. know where _

_ I'd be ___ with - out ___ you here _

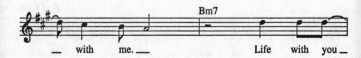

_ with me. ___ Life with you _

friend. ___ Oh, ___ whoa,.

___ ooh, oh. ___ You're my ___ best

friend. Oh, ___ yeah. ___

Ooh, ___

___ you're my ___ best friend.

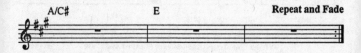

Repeat and Fade

MY NEXT THIRTY YEARS

Words and Music by
PHIL VASSAR

© 1999 EMI APRIL MUSIC INC. and PHIL VASSAR MUSIC
All Rights Controlled and Administered by EMI APRIL MUSIC INC.
All Rights Reserved International Copyright Secured Used by Permission

In my next thir-ty years

I'm gon-na have some fun,

try to for-get a-bout all the

cra-zy things I've done.

May-be now I've con-quered all my ad-o-les-cent fears

and I'll do it bet-ter in my next thir-ty years.

My next thir-ty years I'm gon-na
next thir-ty years will be the

set - tle all ___ the scores, ___
best years of ___ my life. ___

cry a lit-tle less,___ laugh a lit - tle more,
Raise a lit-tle___ fam-i-ly___ and hang out with my wife.

find a world of hap - pi - ness with - out the hate. and fear,
Spend pre-cious mo-ments with the ones that I___ hold dear.

fig - ure out just what I'm do - in' here ___
Make up ___ for lost ___ time ___ here ___

To Coda ⊕

___ in my next thir-ty years.
___ in my next thir-ty

Oh, my next thir-ty years ___

I'm gon - na watch my weight,

eat a few more sal - ads and

not stay up ___ so late.

Drink a lit - tle lem - on - ade ___ and

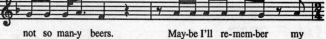

not so man-y beers. May-be I'll re-mem-ber my

D.S. al Coda

next thir - ty years. My

CODA

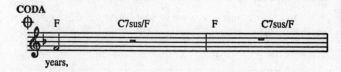

years,

in my next thir - ty years. ___

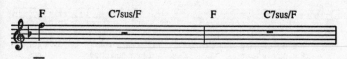

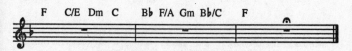

NEON MOON

Words and Music by
RONNIE DUNN

Copyright © 1990 Sony/ATV Songs LLC and Showbilly Music
All Rights Administered by Sony/ATV Music Publishing, 8 Music Square West, Nashville, TN 37203
International Copyright Secured All Rights Resereved

PLEASE REMEMBER ME

Words and Music by RODNEY CROWELL and WILL JENNINGS

Copyright © 1995 Sony/ATV Tunes LLC and Blue Sky Rider Songs
All Rights on behalf of Sony/ATV Tunes LLC Administered by Sony/ATV Music Publishing,
8 Music Square West, Nashville, TN 37203
All Rights on behalf of Blue Sky Rider Songs Administered by Irving Music, Inc.
International Copyright Secured   All Rights Reserved

194

The days keep com - in' with - out
Out in this brave new world you'll

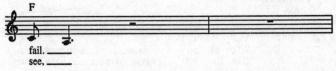

fail. _____
see, _____

A new wind _____ is gon - na
oh, the val - leys and the

find your sail.
peaks.
That's
And I can

where your jour - ney _____ starts.
see you on the _____ top.

You'll _____ find bet - ter love,

strong _____ as it ev - er was,

196

me   when you're out   walk -   ing,

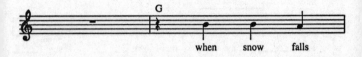

when   snow   falls

high   out - side   your   door,

late   at   night __ when   you're not   sleep -

- in'   and   moon - light

falls   a - cross your   floor

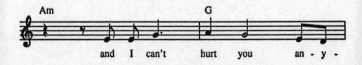

and   I   can't   hurt   you   an - y -

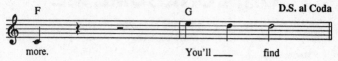

D.S. al Coda

F   G

more.   You'll ___ find

CODA

C   Em7

me.

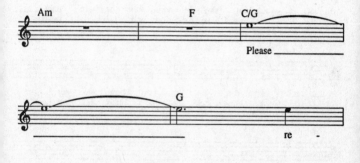

Am   F   C/G

Please ___

G

re -

F

mem - ber me. ___
(Vocal 1st time only)

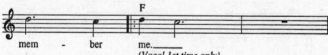

Am7   G/A   F

C   **Repeat and Fade**

OH, LONESOME ME

Words and Music by
DON GIBSON

Copyright © 1958 (Renewed 1986) by Acuff-Rose Music, Inc.
All Rights Reserved   Used by Permission

OKIE FROM MUSKOGEE

Words and Music by MERLE HAGGARD
and ROY EDWARD BURRIS

Copyright © 1969 Sony/ATV Songs LLC
Copyright Renewed
International Copyright Secured All Rights Reserved

And I'm proud to be an O-kie. From Mus-ko-gee; A place where e-ven squares can have a ball. ___

Bb7

We still wave Ol' Glo-ry down at the Court House, White light-ning's still the big-gest thrill of all. ___

Eb

1,2   3

(3.) Leath-er ___

ON THE OTHER HAND

Words and Music by DON SCHLITZ
and PAUL OVERSTREET

Easy Country Swing

On one hand, ___ I count the rea - sons ___ I could
arms I ___ feel the pas - sion ___ I

stay with you, _ and hold you close to
thought had died. _ When I looked in - to your

me all night long So man - y ___ lov - ers'
eyes ___ I found my - self. When I first _ kissed your

games _ I'd love to play with you on that
lips ___ I felt _ so a - live. I've got to

hand there's no rea - son why it's wrong.
hand it to you girl ___ you're some - thing else.

© 1985 SCREEN GEMS-EMI MUSIC INC.,
SCARLET MOON MUSIC, UNIVERSAL - MCA MUSIC PUBLISHING,
A Division of UNIVERSAL STUDIOS, INC. and DON SCHLITZ MUSIC
All Rights for DON SCHLITZ MUSIC Controlled and Administered by
UNIVERSAL - MCA MUSIC PUBLISHING, A Division of UNIVERSAL STUDIOS, INC.
All Rights for SCARLET MOON MUSIC Administered by COPYRIGHT.NET
All Rights Reserved   International Copyright Secured   Used by Permission

RELEASE ME

Words and Music by ROBERT YOUNT,
EDDIE MILLER and DUB WILLIAMS

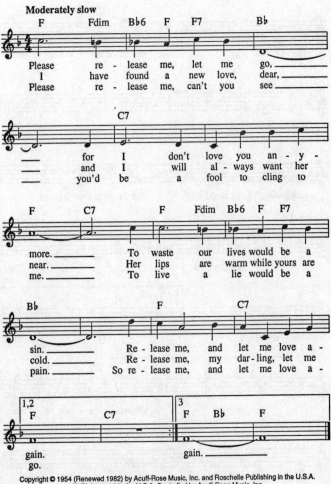

Copyright © 1954 (Renewed 1982) by Acuff-Rose Music, Inc. and Roschelle Publishing in the U.S.A.
All Rights outside the U.S.A. Controlled by Acuff-Rose Music, Inc.
All Rights Reserved   Used by Permission

TOO GONE TOO LONG

Words and Music by
GENE PISTILLI

Moderately, in 2

B7

You've been too gone ___ for
long way go - in' the

too long. ___ It's too late ___ to
wrong way. ___ Don't e - ven set your

E7

come back now.
suit - case down.

You

A

It's been so long since ___ you
want - ed to roam, ___ now ___ you're

walked out my door. ___ Now you're
pay - in' the bills. ___ You're an

D   B7

just an old ___ song ___ no - bod - y
old roll - in' stone who rolled

E

Copyright © 1987 ALMO MUSIC CORP.
All Rights Reserved   Used by Permission

ROCKY TOP

Words and Music by BOUDLEAUX BRYANT
and FELICE BRYANT

1. Wish that I was on ol' Rock-y Top,
2. Once two stran-gers climbed ol' Rock-y Top,

down in the Ten-nes-see hills; Ain't no smog-gy
lookin' for a moon-shine still; Stran-gers ain't come

smoke on Rock-y Top; Ain't no tel-e-phone bills;
down from Rock-y Top; Reckon they nev-er will;

Once I had a girl on Rock-y Top;
Corn won't grow at all on Rock-y Top;
3. *(See additional lyrics)*

Half bear, oth-er half cat; Wild as a mink, but
Dirt's too rock-y by far; That's why all the

Copyright © 1967 by HOUSE OF BRYANT PUBLICATIONS, Gatlinburg, TN
Copyright Renewed
International Copyright Secured   All Rights Reserved

Additional Lyrics

3. I've had years of cramped-up city life
   Trapped like a duck in a pen;
   All I know is it's a pity life
   Can't be simple again.
   Chorus

SWINGIN'

Words and Music by JOHN DAVID ANDERSON and LIONEL DELMORE

Moderately

1. There's ___ a lit-tle girl in our neigh-bor-hood. Her
2.,3. *(See additional lyrics)*

name is Char-lotte John-son, and she's real-ly look-ing good. I

had to go and see her, so I called her on the phone. I walked

[1] o-ver to her house ___ and this was go-in' on: 2. Her

[2,3] **Chorus** A7

love down to my toes. And we was swing-in', ___

E7

(swing-in') yes, we was swing-in', ___

B7

(swing-in') ___ Lit-tle Char-lotte, she's as pret-ty as the

Copyright © 1982 IRVING MUSIC, INC.,
UNIVERSAL - POLYGRAM INTERNATIONAL PUBLISHING, INC. and LIONEL DELMORE MUSIC
All Rights Reserved   Used by Permission

an-gels when they sing. I can't be-lieve I'm out here on her

front porch in the swing, just a swing-in'. ___ (Swing-in' 3. Now

CODA

Lit-tle Char-lotte, she's as pret-ty as the

an-gels when they sing. I can't be-lieve I'm out here on her

front porch in the swing, just a swing-in'. ___

Repeat and Fade

(Swing-in', ___ swing-in'.) ___

Additional Lyrics

2. Her brother was on the sofa
Eatin' chocolate pie.
Her mama was in the kitchen
Cuttin' chicken up to fry.
Her daddy was in the backyard
Rollin' up a garden hose.
I was on the porch with Charlotte
Feelin' love down to my toes.
(Chorus)

3. Now Charlotte, she's darlin';
She's the apple of my eye.
When I'm on the swing with her
It makes me almost high.
And Charlotte is my lover,
And she has been since the spring
I just can't believe it started
On her front porch in the swing.
(Chorus)

TO BE LOVED BY YOU

Words and Music by MIKE REID
and GARY BURR

Copyright © 1995 ALMO MUSIC CORP., BRIO BLUES MUSIC, UNIVERSAL - MCA MUSIC PUBLISHING,
A Division of UNIVERSAL STUDIOS, INC. and GARY BURR MUSIC
All Rights for BRIO BLUES MUSIC Administered by ALMO MUSIC CORP.
All Rights Reserved   Used by Permission

you. *(Instrumental)*

And e - ven when

we're worlds a - part,

just keep this prom - ise in your heart.

(Instrumental)

D.S. al Coda

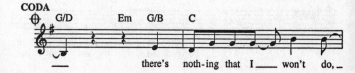

Let the moun-

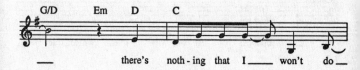

there's noth-ing that I ___ won't do, ___

___ there's noth - ing that I ___ won't do ___

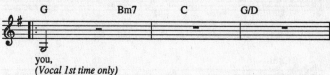

___ to be loved by

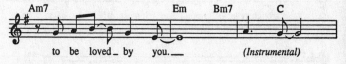

you,
(Vocal 1st time only)

to be loved _ by you. ___ *(Instrumental)*

Repeat and Fade

WALK ON FAITH

Words and Music by MIKE REID
and ALLEN SHAMBLIN

Copyright © 1990 ALMO MUSIC CORP., BRIO BLUES MUSIC and BMG SONGS, INC.
All Rights for BRIO BLUES MUSIC Administered by ALMO MUSIC CORP.
All Rights Reserved Used by Permission

— there — from here ——— is to } walk — on
— to — ar - rive ——— when we }

faith, ——— trust — in love. ———

Just keep on put-ting one — foot down — in front of the oth-

- er. ——— When the val - ley's — so wide, —

——— we stum-ble — in stride, ———

ev-'ry-thing — in - side ——— wants — to give up. ———

Walk on faith, ——— trust — in

love. ——— Far-ther on — Walk — on

WALKIN' AFTER MIDNIGHT

Lyrics by DON HECHT
Music by ALAN W. BLOCK

Copyright © 1956 (Renewed 1984) by Acuff-Rose Music, Inc.
All Rights Reserved Used by Permission

walk - in'___ af - ter mid-night, search - in' for

you. I stop to

see a weep-in' wil-low cry-in' on his pil-low.

May - be he's cry - in' for me. And

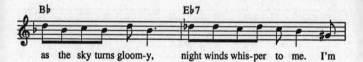

as the sky turns gloom-y, night winds whis-per to me. I'm

lone - ly as lone - ly as can be. I'll go out

CODA

me.

THE WAY YOU LOVE ME

Words and Music by MICHAEL DULANEY
and KEITH FOLLESE

If I could grant you one wish, I
It's not right, it's not fair,

wish you could see the way you kiss.
what you're miss - ing o - ver there.

Ooh, I love watch - ing you, ba - by,
Some - day I'll find a way to show you

when you're driv - ing me, ooh, cra - zy.
just how luck - y I am to know you.

Ooh, I love the way you, love the way you love me.

There's no - where else I'd rath - er be.

Copyright © 1999 by Airstream Dreams Music, Coyote House Music,
Famous Music Corporation, Encore Entertainment, LLC d/b/a
Scott And Soda Music and Follazoo Crew Music (administered by Encore Entertainment)
International Copyright Secured All Rights Reserved

Ooh, to feel the way _ I feel with your arms _ a-round_me.

I on - ly wish_ that you _ could

see _____ the way_ you love _ me.

Whoa, _____ the way _ you

love me.

love me. You're the mil - lion

rea - sons why there's love re - flect - ing

222

A   **D.S. al Coda**

in   my   eyes. _____

CODA

E   B

love   me.

C#m   A

Whoa, _____ the way __ you

E   B   C#m   A

love   me.   Whoa, _____ the way ____

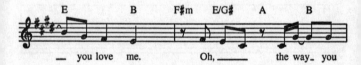

E   B   F#m   E/G#   A   B

__ you love   me.   Oh, _____ the way_ you

E   B   C#m   A

love   me.   The way_ you love   me.

Repeat ad lib. and Fade

E   B   C#m   A

Ooh,   I   love the way_ you love   me.

WHERE THE GREEN GRASS GROWS

Words and Music by **JESS LEARY**
and **CRAIG WISEMAN**

Copyright © 1997 by Song Matters, Inc., Famous Music Corporation,
Daddy Rabbit Music and Almo Music Corp.
International Copyright Secured   All Rights Reserved

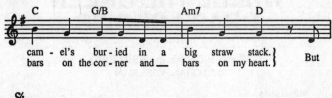

| C | G/B | Am7 | D |

cam - el's bur - ied in a big straw stack. }
bars on the cor - ner and __ bars on my heart. } But

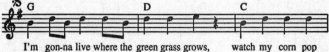

| G | D | C |

I'm gon-na live where the green grass grows, watch my corn pop

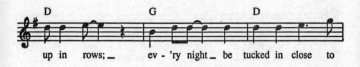

| D | G | D |

up in rows; __ ev - 'ry night __ be tucked in close to

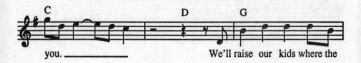

| C | D | G |

you. _____ We'll raise our kids where the

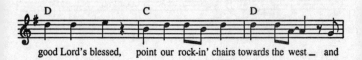

| D | C | D |

good Lord's blessed, point our rock-in' chairs towards the west __ and

To Coda ⊕

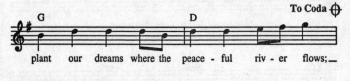

| G | D |

plant our dreams where the peace - ful riv - er flows; __

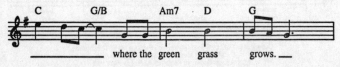

| C | G/B | Am7 | D | G |

_____ where the green grass grows. __

225

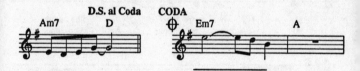

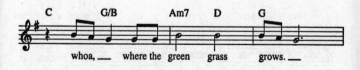

whoa, ___ where the green grass grows. ___

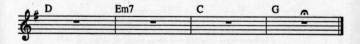

WE DANCED

Words and Music by BRAD PAISLEY
and CHRIS DuBOIS

The bar was emp — ty. I was
- ment there was

— sweep-in' up the floor.
- nev-er an-y doubt

That's when she walked in. I said, "I'm
I had found the one that I had

sor — ry, but we're closed." She said,
al — ways dreamed a-bout. And then one

"I know, but I'm a-
eve-nin' when she stopped

fraid I left my purse." I said, "I
by af-ter work, I

© 1999 EMI APRIL MUSIC INC. and SEA GAYLE MUSIC
All Rights Controlled and Administered by EMI APRIL MUSIC INC.
All Rights Reserved International Copyright Secured Used by Permission

228

di - tion."_____ }
di - tion."_____ }

And we danced.

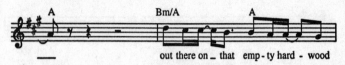

_____ out there on __ that emp - ty hard - wood

floor.____ The chairs up and the lights_turned way down.

____ low. ____ The mu-sic played,_ we held_each oth-er close.

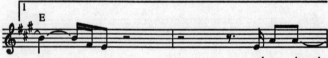

1.

and we danced._

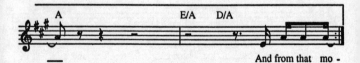

____ And from that mo -

2.

and we danced ____

like no one else had ev-er danced before.

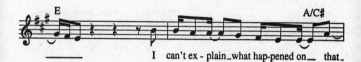

I can't ex - plain what hap-pened on that

floor, but the

mu - sic played, we held each oth -

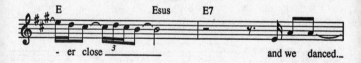

- er close and we danced.

Yeah, we danced.

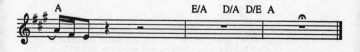

WHAT ABOUT NOW

Words and Music by RON HARBIN,
ANTHONY SMITH and AARON BARKER

The sign ____ in the win-dow said "for sale or trade" on the last ____ re-main-ing din-o-saur De-troit made. ____ Sev-en hun-dred dol-lars was a heck of a deal ____ for a four-hun-dred horse-pow-er juke-box on wheels. And that road ____ rolls ____ out like a wel-come mat. ____ I don't know-tin' this off, ____ ba-by, long e-nough. ____ Just ____ give

Copyright © 2000 Sony/ATV Tunes LLC, Ron Harbin Music, O-Tex Music,
Blind Sparrow Music, WB Music Corp. and Notes To Music
All Rights on behalf of Sony/ATV Tunes LLC and Ron Harbin Music Administered by
Sony/ATV Music Publishing, 8 Music Square West, Nashville, TN 37203
All Rights on behalf of Blind Sparrow Music Administered by O-Tex Music
International Copyright Secured   All Rights Reserved

B
_ where it goes,_ but it beats_ where we're at._ We al -
_ me the word and we'll be kick-in' up dust._ We_

A
- ways said _ some - day, _ some - how_ we're gon - na
_ both know_ it's just a mat - ter of time_ till our_

B   N.C.
get a - way_ gon-na blow_ this town._ }
hearts start rac - in' for that coun-ty line._ }   What a-bout now?_

E   B
_   How 'bout to - night?_   Ba - by, for once_

C#m7   A
_ let's don't_ think_ twice. _____   Let's take_

E   B
_ that spin_ that nev - er ends_ that_ we've_

C#m7   A   B
_ been talk - in' a - bout._   What a-bout now?_

this town— for - ev - er mak - in' plans,—

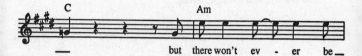

but there won't ev - er be—

a— bet - ter time— to take— this chance.—

What a-bout now?—

CODA

What a-bout now?—

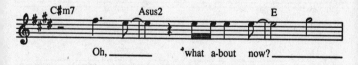

Oh, _____ what a-bout now? _____

WHY ME?
(Why Me, Lord?)

Words and Music by
KRIS KRISTOFFERSON

© 1972 (Renewed 2000) RESACA MUSIC PUBLISHING CO.
All Rights Controlled and Administered by EMI BLACKWOOD MUSIC INC.
All Rights Reserved   International Copyright Secured   Used by Permission

WILD ANGELS

Words and Music by GARY HARRISON, MATRACA BERG and HARRY STINSON

Moderately

Be-tween the per-fect world _ and the bot-tom line, _ keep-ing love a-live _ in these trou-bled times, _ well, it's a mir-a-cle in it-self. _ And we know too well _ what that's a-bout. _ Still, we made it through; _ on-ly

must-'ve been hard, it must-'ve been tough keep-ing up _ with cra-zy fools like us, _ 'cause it's so eas-y to fall a-part. _ And we still break _ each oth-er's heart some-times, _ spend some nights _ on the

© 1995 EMI LONGITUDE MUSIC CO., GREAT BROAD MUSIC,
AUGUST WIND MUSIC, SONY/ATV SONGS LLC and GEORGIAN HILLS MUSIC
All Rights for GEORGIAN HILLS MUSIC Controlled and Administered by EMI LONGITUDE MUSIC
All Rights for SONY/ATV SONGS LLC Administered by
SONY/ATV MUSIC PUBLISHING, 8 Music Square West, Nashville, TN 37203
All Rights Reserved   International Copyright Secured   Used by Permission

238

- gels, _____ wild _____ an -

- gels, _____ ba - by, what _____

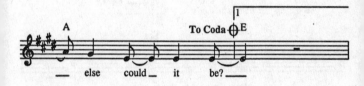

_____ else could _____ it be? _____

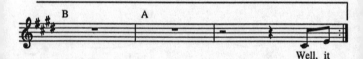

Well, it

_____ There are _____ some nights _____

_____ I watch you while _____ you dream. _____

_____ I swear I hear the

sound ... of beat-ing wings.

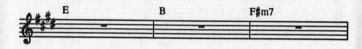

Oh, it must-'ve been

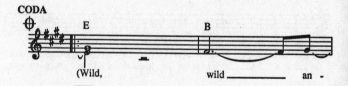

(Wild, ... wild ____ an -

- gels.) ____

WITHOUT YOU

**Words and Music by NATALIE MAINES
and ERIC SILVER**

I've sure en-joyed _____ the rain, _____
nev-er thought _____ I'd be

but I'm look-in' for-ward to
ly-ing here with-out _____ you by _____

the sun. You have to feel _____ the pain
my side. _____ It seems un-real _____ to me

when you lose the love _____ you gave
that the life you prom-ised was

some-one. I thought by now the time _____ would take a-way _____
a lie. _____ You make it look so eas-y mak-ing love _____

these lone _____ ly tears. _____
in-to mem-o-ries. _____

© 1999 SCRAPIN' TOAST MUSIC (ASCAP)/Administered by BUG MUSIC,
EMI APRIL MUSIC INC. and 703 MUSIC
All Rights for 703 MUSIC Controlled and Administered by EMI APRIL MUSIC INC.
All Rights Reserved   Used by Permission

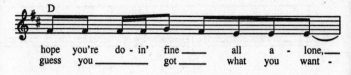

hope you're do-in' fine ___ all a - lone, ___
guess you ___ got ___ what you want -

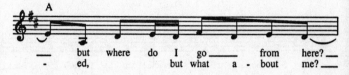

___ but where do I go ___ from here? ___
- ed, but what a - bout me? ___

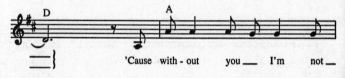

___ } 'Cause with - out you ___ I'm not

___ o - kay. ___ And with-out you ___ I've lost ___

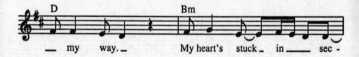

___ my way. ___ My heart's stuck ___ in ___ sec -

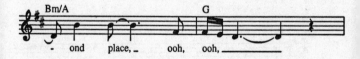

- ond place, ___ ooh, ooh, ___

To Coda ⊕ D

with - out ___ you. ___

XXX'S AND OOO'S
(An American Girl)

Words and Music by ALICE RANDALL
and MATRACA BERG

Copyright © 1994 Sony/ATV Tunes LLC, Mother Dixie Songs,
EMI Longitude Music, Great Broad Music and August Wind Music
All Rights on behalf of Sony/ATV Tunes LLC and Mother Dixie Songs Administered by
Sony/ATV Music Publishing, 8 Music Square West, Nashville, TN 37203
International Copyright Secured   All Rights Reserved

pic - ture of her mom - ma in ___ heels and ___ pearls.

She's {(D.S.) tryin' to / gon-na} make it in her dad - dy's world. She's an A -

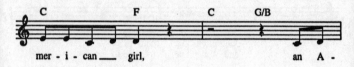

mer - i - can ___ girl, an A -

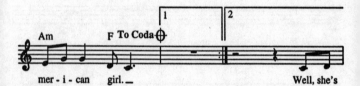

mer - i - can girl. ___ Well, she's

got her God and she's got good wine, A -

re - tha Frank - lin and Pat - sy Cline. ___

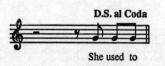

D.S. al Coda

She used to

CODA

She's an A -

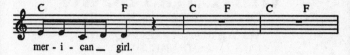

mer - i - can __ girl.

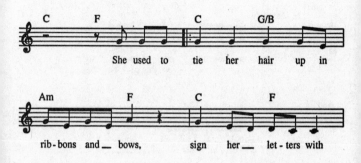

She used to tie her hair up in

rib - bons and __ bows, sign her __ let - ters with

X - 's and O's. Got a pic - ture of her mom - ma in __

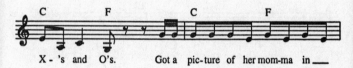

heels and __ pearls. She's gon - na make it in her

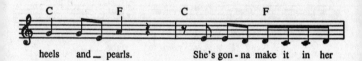

dad - dy's world. She's an A - mer - i - can __ girl, yeah. __

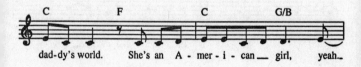

Repeat and Fade

But she'd

WRITE THIS DOWN

Words and Music by KENT ROBBINS
and DANA HUNT

I nev-er saw the end in ___ sight; ___
bot-tom of the page. ___

fools are kind of blind. ___
I'll swear un-der oath.

Thought ev-'ry-thing was go-in' all right,
'Cause ev-'ry sin-gle word ___ is true, ___

but I was run-nin' out of time. ___
and I think you need to know. ___

'Cause you had one foot out the door.
So use it as a book - mark, ___

I swear I did-n't see. ___
stick it on your 'frig-er-a-tor door,

Copyright © 1997, 1998 IRVING MUSIC, INC., COLTER BAY MUSIC and NEON SKY MUSIC
All Rights Reserved   Used by Permission

But if you're real-ly go-in' a-way,_
here's some fi-nal words from me.__

hang it in a pic-ture frame up a-bove the
man-tle where you'll see it for sure.__

Ba-by, write this down,_ take_ a lit-tle
note to re-mind_ you in case you did-n't

know. Tell your-self I love you and I don't want you to
go._ Write this down._

Take my words_ and read_ 'em ev-'ry

248

YOUR CHEATIN' HEART

Words and Music by
HANK WILLIAMS

Copyright © 1952 (Renewed 1980) by Acuff-Rose Music, Inc. and Hiriam Music in the U.S.A.
All Rights for Hiriam Music Administered by Rightsong Music Inc.
All Rights outside the U.S.A. Controlled by Acuff-Rose Music, Inc.
International Copyright Secured   All Rights Reserved

GUITAR CHORD FRAMES

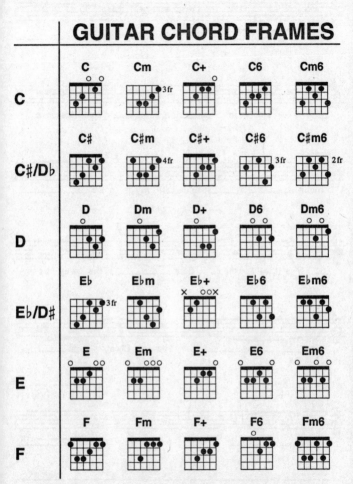

This guitar chord reference includes 120 commonly used chords. For a more complete guide to guitar chords, see "THE PAPERBACK CHORD BOOK" (HL00702009).

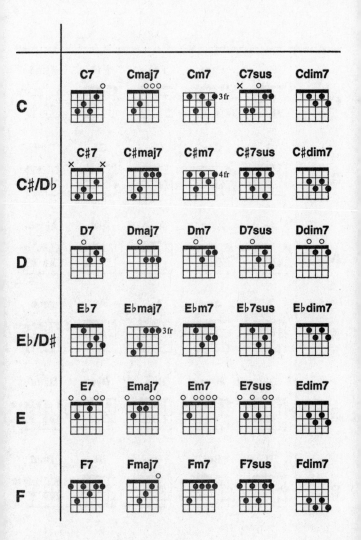

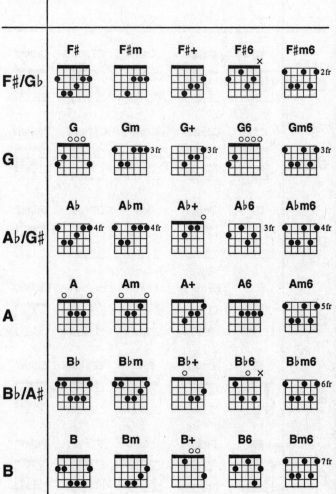

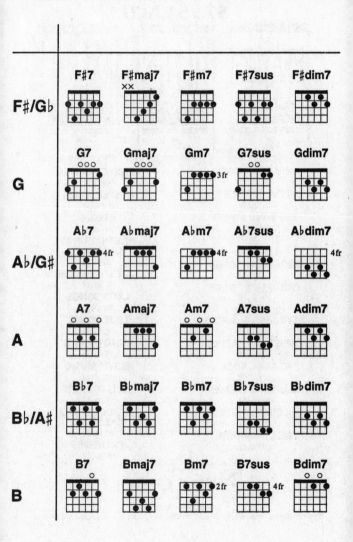

THE PAPERBACK SONGS SERIES

$7.95 EACH

'80s & '90s ROCK
00240126

THE BEATLES
00702008

BIG BAND SWING
00240171

THE BLUES
00702014

BROADWAY SONGS
00240157

CHILDREN'S SONGS
00240149

**CHORDS FOR
KEYBOARD & GUITAR**
00702009

CHRISTMAS CAROLS
00240142

CLASSIC ROCK
00310058

CLASSICAL THEMES
00240160

COUNTRY HITS
00702013

NEIL DIAMOND
00702012

GOOD OL' SONGS
00240159

GOSPEL SONGS
00240143

HYMNS
00240103

**INTERNATIONAL
FOLKSONGS**
00240144

JAZZ STANDARDS
00240114

LATIN SONGS
00240156

LOVE SONGS
00240150

MOTOWN HITS
00240125

MOVIE MUSIC
00240113

ELVIS PRESLEY
00240102

**THE ROCK & ROLL
COLLECTION**
00702020

TV THEMES
00240170

For More Information, See Your Local Music Dealer,
Or Write To:

**HAL•LEONARD®
CORPORATION**
7777 W. BLUEMOUND RD. P.O. BOX 13819 MILWAUKEE, WI 53213

www.halleonard.com

Prices, availability and contents subject to change without notice. Some products may not be available outside the U.S.A.

0601